Student Interactive

myView
LITERACY
1

SAVVAS
LEARNING COMPANY

Cover: 854140/Shutterstock; 123RF; Jps/Shutterstock; Elena Shchipkova/123RF; Chones/Shutterstock; Eric Isselee/Shutterstock; RTimages/Shutterstock; 123RF; Kamenetskiy Konstantin/Shutterstock; Coprid/Shutterstock; Dencg/Shutterstock; Eric Isselee/Shutterstock; Vitalii Tiahunov/123RF; StevenRussellSmithPhotos/Shutterstock; Alena Brozova/Shutterstock; Avelkrieg/123RF; Magnia/Shutterstock

Attributions of third party content appear on pages 258–259 which constitutes an extension of this copyright page.

ISBN-13: 978-0-134-90879-3
ISBN-10: 0-134-90879-1

6 21

Julie Coiro, Ph.D.

Jim Cummins, Ph.D.

Pat Cunningham, Ph.D.

Elfrieda Hiebert, Ph.D.

Pamela Mason, Ed.D.

Ernest Morrell, Ph.D.

P. David Pearson, Ph.D.

Frank Serafini, Ph.D.

Alfred Tatum, Ph.D.

Sharon Vaughn, Ph.D.

Judy Wallis, Ed.D.

Lee Wright, Ed.D.

Beyond My World

Beyond My World

Essential Question

How do the seasons affect us?

▶ **Watch**

"Four Fun Seasons" See how the four seasons are different.

🦉 **TURN** *and* **TALK** How can you describe each season?

SAVVAS
realize™
Go ONLINE for
all lessons.

▶ VIDEO

🔊 AUDIO

🎮 GAME

✏ ANNOTATE

📖 BOOK

🔍 RESEARCH

Reading Workshop

Reading-Writing Bridge

- Academic Vocabulary
- Read Like a Writer, Write for a Reader
- Spelling • Language and Conventions

Writing Workshop

How-To Book

- Plan Your How-To Book
- Create Simple Graphics • Features and Simple Graphics
- Edit for Punctuation Marks • Publish and Celebrate

Project-Based Inquiry

- Inquire • Research • Collaborate

Independent Reading

Select a book to read on your own. Each time you read, try reading for a longer period of time. It may be helpful to check a clock or use a timer. After you read, you can meet with friends to tell about your book.

 **MY TURN** Use this list to get ready to tell about your book.

1. **Think** about what you are reading.

I think _____

_____

2. **Talk** about what you read with a partner. Remember to:
   • take turns speaking.
   • listen to each other.
   • ask each other questions.

3. **Share** your ideas with the class.

My Reading Log

Date	Book	Pages Read	Minutes Read	My Ratings
				☺ ☺ ☹
				☺ ☺ ☹
				☺ ☺ ☹
				☺ ☺ ☹
				☺ ☺ ☹

You may wish to use a Reader's Notebook to record and respond to your reading.

Unit Goals

In this unit, you will:

- read informational texts.
- write a how-to book.
- learn about the seasons.

 MY TURN **Color** the pictures to answer.

I can read informational texts.	👍	👎
I can make and use words to read and write informational text.	👍	👎
I can write a how-to book.	👍	👎
I understand the seasons.	👍	👎

Academic Vocabulary

sense	expect	process	information

Using academic vocabulary helps you talk about ideas in meaningful ways.

In this unit, you will learn **information** about the seasons. How can you use each **sense** to **process** what to **expect** during the seasons?

TURN and TALK Use the Academic Vocabulary words to talk with a partner about the picture.

Seasons of an Apple Tree

Spring
Apple trees begin to sprout leaves and flowers from their branches.

Winter
In some places, apple trees rest during the winter. The cold gets the trees ready for another growing season.

What happens during the seasons?

Summer

The apples begin to grow and change color. But they are not ready yet.

Autumn

The fruit is ready! People pick the apples from the trees. It's time for lots of good treats!

TURNand**TALK** Discuss how the apple trees are similar and different during the seasons.

Middle and Final Sounds

SEE and SAY Say each sound as you name each picture. Then say the picture name again.

boot

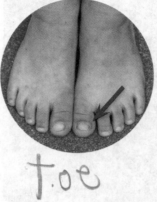
toe

Crow

Long o Spelled oa, ow, oe

The long **o** sound is spelled **oa** in **boat**.
The long **o** sound is spelled **ow** in **crow**.
The long **o** sound is spelled **oe** in **toe**.

MY TURN Read these words.

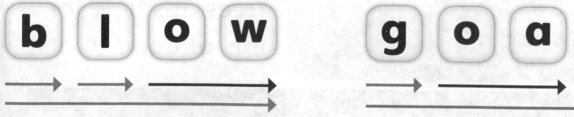

b l o w   g o a l

Long o Spelled oa, ow, oe

TURN and TALK Read these long **o** words.

coat	doe	row

road	tow	snow

MY TURN Say the picture name. Circle the word that names the picture. Then read the word.

(soap)   sap   get   (goat)

top   (toe)   brow   (bowl)

Read Together

Long o Spelled oa, ow, oe

MY TURN Use the words to finish the sentences. Then read the sentences.

slow	boat	toad	blow

Joe floats a _boat_ in the pond.

Will the breeze _blow_ the boat?

A _slow_ breeze moves the boat.

Joe spots a _toad_ in the pond.

MY TURN Write a sentence about the boat.

The boat is floting away.

Segment and Blend Sounds

SEE and SAY Sometimes you hear more than one consonant sound at the beginning of a word. Segment the sounds in each picture by saying each sound. Then blend the sounds to say the picture name again.

Consonant Blends and Trigraphs

Three consonants at the beginning of a word are spelled together and make a blended sound, like the **thr** in throw and the **spl** in **split**.

MY TURN Read the word.

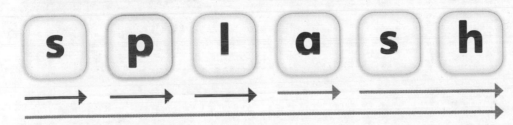

s   p   l   a   s   h

My Words to Know

Some words you must remember and practice.

MY TURN Read these words.

buy	about	would	write	people

MY TURN Complete each sentence with a word from the box.

Handwriting Print the answers legibly, or clearly. Leave spaces between the words.

1. Dave watches _people_ feed birds.

2. Dave _____ like to feed them.

3. Where can he _____ seeds?

4. He will _____ _____ birds.

Read Together

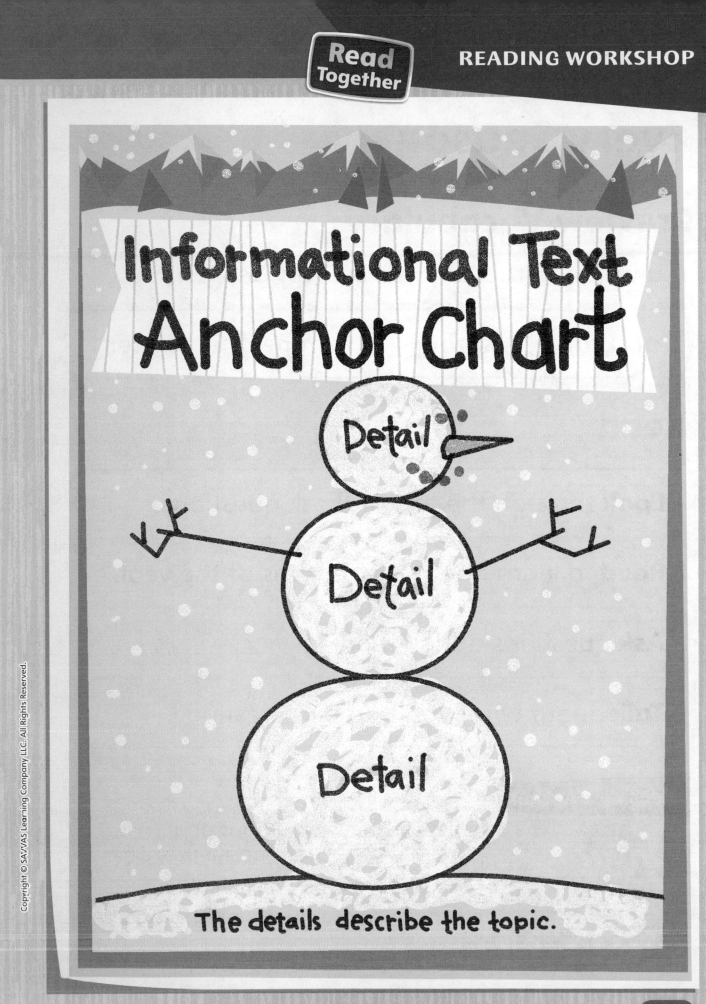

Informational Text Anchor Chart

Detail

Detail

Detail

The details describe the topic.

Every Season

Preview Vocabulary

You will read these words in *Every Season.*

| autumn | spring | summer | winter |

Read

Look through the text and ask questions.

Read to learn about the seasons of the year.

Ask questions during reading.

Talk about what you found interesting.

Meet the Author

Shelley Rotner is an author and photographer of over 30 children's books. She hopes to help children talk openly about their thoughts and feelings.

AUDIO

Audio with Highlighting

ANNOTATE

Every Season

Shelley Rotner and Anne Love Woodhull
Photographs by Shelley Rotner

I Love Spring

when grass grows green.

Speckled eggs
fill woven nests.

Showers soak.

Seeds sprout.

Flowers bloom.

CLOSE READ

<u>Underline</u> the words the author uses to describe spring.

Crocuses pop.
Daffodils open,
then
lilacs **s p r e a d**
their sweet smell.
Salamanders
slither out
from under mossy
rocks.
Ducklings follow,
all in a row.

We hold rabbits,
lambs,
puppies,
and chicks.
Spring
is the time
to dig
and plant.
But then summer comes, and ...

CLOSE READ

Highlight a detail that connects to
a personal experience you have had
in spring.

I Love Summer Too

The sun
shines strong
and hot.
You can wear
a straw hat, or
go barefoot
in the grass.

Bees sip,
frogs hop,
butterflies
f l u t t e r
and
land.

We taste strawberries, lemonade,
watermelon, ice cream.

CLOSE READ

<u>Underline</u> the words the author uses to
describe summer.

Shorebirds scurry and peck.
I hear the
roar
of ocean waves.
Summer is the time to splash
and swim.
But then autumn
comes and ...

I Love Autumn Too

Wind whips,
seeds
s c a t t e r.

We pull up
our hoods
and zip up
our jackets.
Leaves turn
and

fall.

Orange maple, red oak,
yellow ash.

We pick pumpkins,

taste apples,

pears,

and pies.

CLOSE READ

Highlight a detail about autumn that connects to a personal experience you have had.

Geese honk
and head south.
Chipmunks
store acorns
in a secret
spot.
Autumn
is the time
to rake
and
jump.
But then winter comes, and ...

I Love Winter Too

The cold brings icicles
and snowflakes
that swirl.

CLOSE READ

Underline the words the author uses to
describe autumn.

We make snow angels
then sip hot chocolate.
Mmmm ...
Horses grow thick coats
to keep warm.
Chickadees search
for seeds.

Snow blankets
branches
and buds.
Animals leave their t r a c k s.

VOCABULARY IN CONTEXT

Words and pictures can help you learn
what an unknown word means. Underline
the words that help you understand
what **tracks** are. How does the picture
help you?

We wear hats,

mittens,

scarves,

and skates.

Winter is the time to coast and slide.

But then spring comes, and ...

I Love Spring

Develop Vocabulary

MY TURN Write a word from the box to label each picture.

autumn	spring	summer	winter

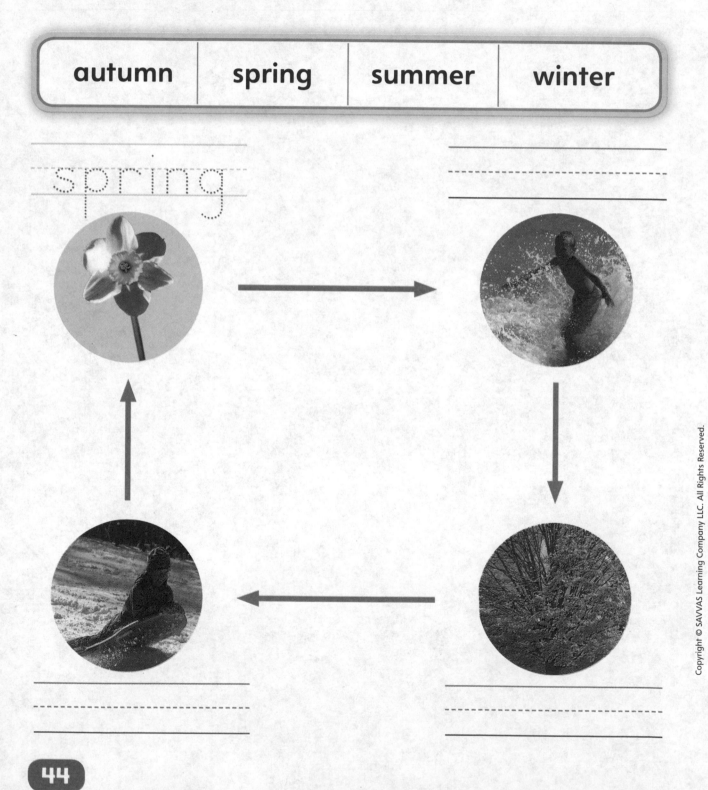

spring

Check for Understanding

MY TURN Write the answers to the questions. You can look back at the text.

1. How do the pictures help you know this is informational text?

_____

_____

_____

_____

2. Why does the author use a lot of photos for each season?

_____

_____

_____

_____

3. How are the seasons similar? Use text evidence.

_____

_____

_____

_____

Find Text Structure

Informational texts have an organizational pattern, or the way the information is presented. The information can describe a topic.

MY TURN Write a word or phrase to describe these seasons. Look back at what you underlined in the text.

spring _____

summer _____

autumn _____

TURN and TALK Discuss how these descriptions support the authors' reason for writing the text.

Make Connections

Readers make connections when they find ways to relate to a text. They can make connections to personal experiences.

MY TURN Draw and describe your experiences in these seasons. Use what you highlighted in the text.

Spring	Autumn

Reflect and Share

Talk About It

You read an informational text that describes each season. How is the structure of this text similar to other texts you have read about the seasons?

- -

Share Information and Ideas

When talking with others, it is important to:

- Speak clearly.
- Use complete sentences.

Use the words on the note to help you share ideas with others.

I think . . .

Now share your ideas with others.

- -

Weekly Question

What happens during the seasons?

Read Together

I can make and use words to read and write informational text.

My Learning Goal

Academic Vocabulary

Related words share the same base word or root. Knowing the meaning of one word can give you clues about the meanings of related words.

MY TURN Read each sentence. <u>Underline</u> the word that is related to the bold word.

1. **information**

   Lee will <u>inform</u> his friends about the party.

2. **sense**

   I have a funny sensation in my nose.

3. **expect**

   The ending of that show was unexpected.

4. **process**

   The food in this meal is all unprocessed.

Read Like a Writer, Write for a Reader

Authors organize information in a text to support their reason for writing.

I LOVE **AUTUMN** TOO
Wind whips,
seeds
scatter.

The author informs readers by describing what happens in autumn.

TURN and **TALK** Find another example from the text where the author uses description. Talk about how the description supports the author's purpose.

MY TURN Write a sentence that describes a season you want to inform readers about.

_____

_____

_____

_____

I can write a how-to book.

My Learning Goal

How-To Book

A how-to book is a procedural text. It gives directions on how to make or do something. It has:

- numbered steps in order.
- pictures that show what to do.

Building a Snowman

1. **Roll** a small, medium, and large snowball.

2. **Stack** the snowballs.

3. **Add** a face and buttons.

4. **Add** a hat and stick arms.

Steps

Generate Ideas

A **topic** is what an author writes about. Authors choose a topic they know a lot about.

MY TURN What do you know how to do or make really well? Brainstorm some topics for your how-to book.

_____

- -

_____

- -

_____

- -

_____

MY TURN (Circle) the topic you like best. Draw a picture of what you will write about.

Plan Your How-To Book

TURN and TALK Plan your how-to book by telling your idea to your Writing Club. Follow these steps when it is your turn.

1. Name what you will do or make.

2. Tell the steps in order.

3. Describe the pictures you will include.

4. Ask if anyone has questions.

5. Answer questions in complete sentences.

6. Listen to others' ideas for their how-to books.

Read Together

Seasons Here and There

What season is it in different parts of the world? Check a Web site! A Web site has digital features, such as videos and a search bar. A Web site can be multimodal—it has a combination of words, pictures, videos, and sounds.

www.url.here

It's winter here!

Chicago, Illinois, U.S.A.

What are seasons like around the world?

MY TURN Circle the digital and multimodal features on this Web site.

Q Search

Date

Sydney, Australia

It's summer here!

N
W E
S

Different Sounds

 **SEE and SAY** Say the name of each picture. Listen for the vowel sound. Tell which picture name has the long **u** sound. Tell which picture name has the short **u** sound.

Long i Spelled igh

The letters **igh** make the long **i** sound in **tight**.

MY TURN Read these words.

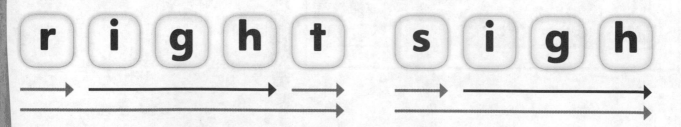

Long i Spelled igh

TURN and TALK Decode these words.

right	bright	fright
light	sight	flight
sigh	night	flashlight
high	tight	nightlight

MY TURN Write **igh** to finish the words. Then read the sentences.

1. I like the br**igh**t sunl__i__**gh**t.

2. She likes the stars at n__i__**gh**t.

Long i Spelled igh

MY TURN Read the sentences. <u>Underline</u> the words with the long **i** sound spelled **igh.**

<u>Dwight</u> looks out at <u>night</u>.

He grips his flashlight tight.

It is very bright.

The light helps his sight.

Listen for the sound you hear in **right**.

MY TURN Write another sentence about Dwight using a word with long **i** spelled **igh.**

Dwight

Segment and Blend Sounds

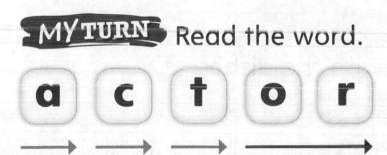 **SEE and SAY** What is each person's job?
Say each sound as you name each picture.
Then say the picture names again.

Suffixes -er, -or

A suffix is a word part added to the end of a
word to make a new word.
The suffixes **-er** and **-or** mean "one who ____."
Reader means "one who reads."
Sailor means "one who sails."

MY TURN Read the word.

a   c   t   o   r

My Words to Know

Some words you must remember and practice.

MY TURN Read these words.

done	once	upon	wash	water

MY TURN Use these words to complete the sentences. Read the sentences.

1. Tell me about a place you went ___once___ .

2. Did you _____ the dishes

   in the _____ ?

3. I am _____ with the dishes.

4. Then sit _____ the couch. I will tell you.

Read Together

Suffixes -er, -or

 **TURN and TALK** Read these words.

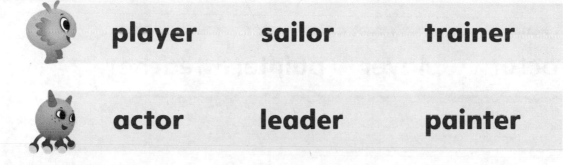

player	sailor	trainer

actor	leader	painter

MY TURN Say each picture name.
Draw a line to match the picture with the word that names the picture.

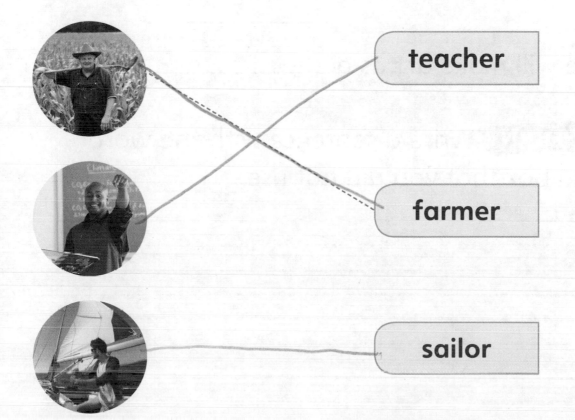

teacher

farmer

sailor

Read Together

Suffixes -er, -or

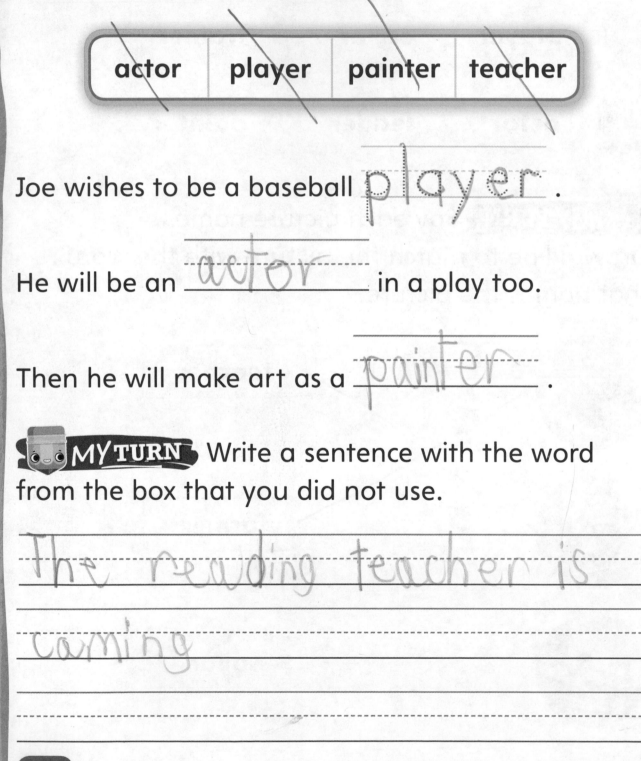

MY TURN Complete the sentences by adding the correct words from the box.

actor	player	painter	teacher

Joe wishes to be a baseball ~~player~~.

He will be an ~~actor~~ in a play too.

Then he will make art as a ~~painter~~.

MY TURN Write a sentence with the word from the box that you did not use.

The reading teacher is coming

The Sailor

Jen got up at the sight of sunlight.

She met the sailor at the dock.

He sat upon his boat.

It is on the water.

AUDIO

Audio with Highlighting

ANNOTATE

Read the story. Highlight the two words with the long i sound.

Jen helped the sailor wash his boat.

"I went far away as an actor," the sailor said.

Highlight the three words with the suffix -or.

He was a <u>painter</u> once.

He was a <u>teacher</u> helping kids.

Jen leaves the dock when the day is done.

<u>Underline</u> the two words with the suffix **-er.**

My Learning Goal

I can read informational text.

SPOTLIGHT ON GENRE

Informational Text

An informational text can have text features. Text features help readers find and learn information. A label names what is in a picture.

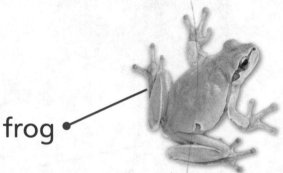

frog

Set a Purpose Readers set a purpose before they begin reading. They think of a reason for reading a text.

TURN and TALK Look at the title and pictures before reading this week's text. Talk about a purpose, or reason, for reading the text.

Informational Text Anchor Chart

Text Features

Picture →

Label → Tree

Seasons Around the World

Preview Vocabulary

You will read these words in *Seasons Around the World*.

dry	rain	snow	sunlight

Read

Look at the text features. Make a prediction about the text.

Read to learn about seasons around the world.

Ask questions during reading.

Talk about what you found interesting.

Meet *the* Author

Ana Galán is an author of books written in both English and Spanish. She was born in Spain and later moved to the United States. Ana loves animals, especially dogs!

Read Together

Genre Informational Text

Seasons Around the World

written by Ana Galán

AUDIO

Audio with Highlighting

ANNOTATE

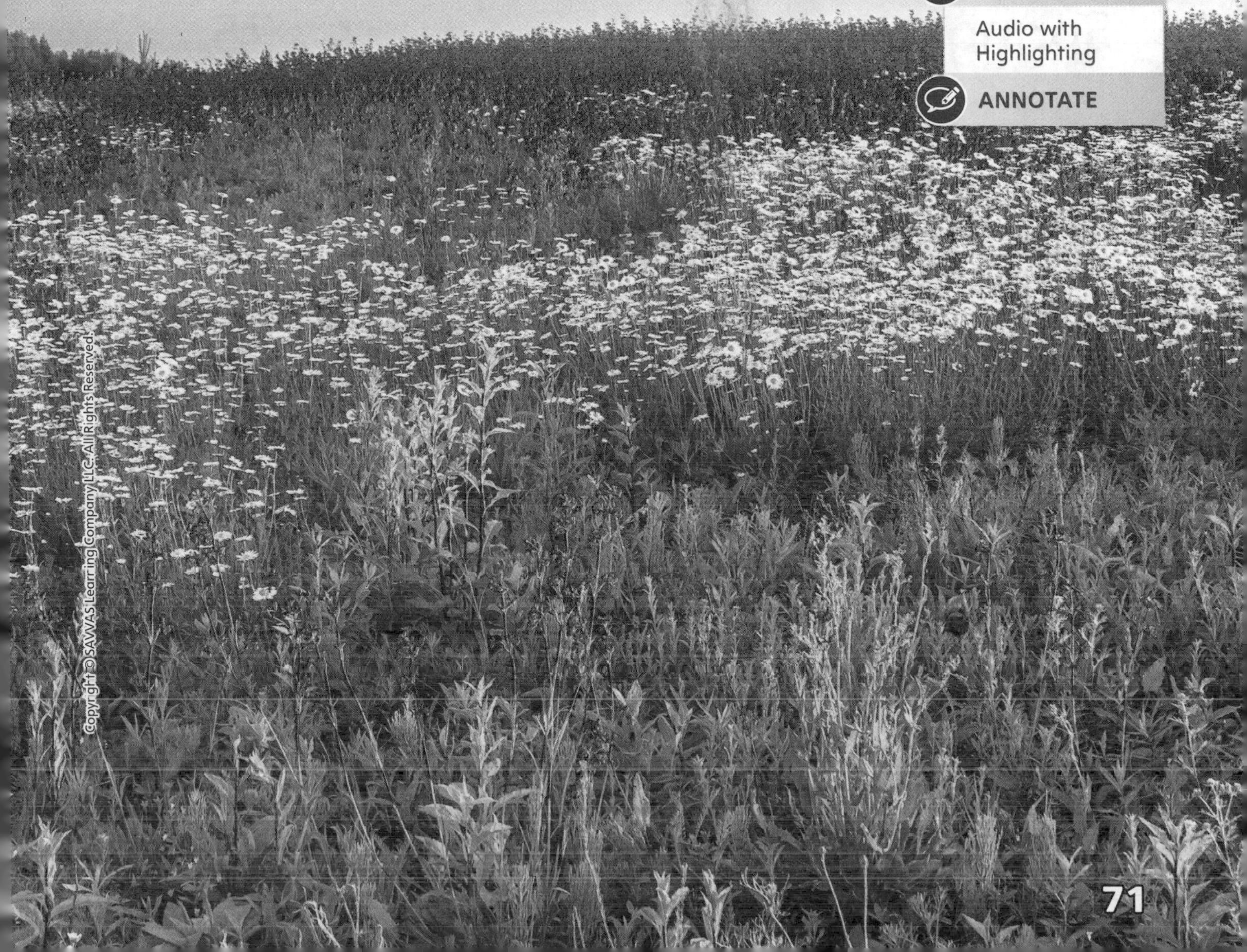

Table of Contents

WINTER

During winter, the days are shorter than they are during other seasons. In many places, the air gets cold and it snows. Most plants and trees stop growing. Some die. Some animals hibernate.

CLOSE READ

Highlight the words that help you make a prediction about the text.

NORWAY

Near the North Pole, the sun never shines in winter. It is dark all day!

SPRING

Spring comes after winter. In many places, baby animals are born. Flowers bloom and leaves appear on the trees. It can rain a lot during spring. The rain and warmer weather help plants grow.

CLOSE READ

Underline the information that the picture and graphic on page 74 help you understand.

Did You Know?

In some parts of the world, there are only two seasons: a rainy season and a dry season!

UGANDA

EQUATOR

The seasons don't change much near the equator. Spring is like all the other seasons.

SUMMER

During summer, the days are longer than they are during other seasons. The sunlight helps plants grow in the summer. People like to spend time in the sun too.

CLOSE READ

Highlight the words that make you change or confirm a prediction you have about this text.

ANTARCTICA

This is the coldest place on Earth. Even in summer, it never gets warm here.

FALL

During fall, the days start to get shorter again. The leaves on some trees change colors and drop to the ground. Animals start getting ready for winter too. They eat a lot. Some animals store food.

Did You Know?

Some butterflies travel all the way from the United States to Mexico in the fall so they can stay warm in winter!

MEXICO

In fall, many birds and animals move to warmer places where they can find food.

Index

CLOSE READ

Underline the information that the picture and graphic on page 80 help you understand.

Develop Vocabulary

 **MY TURN** Draw a line from each word to the picture that shows the meaning.

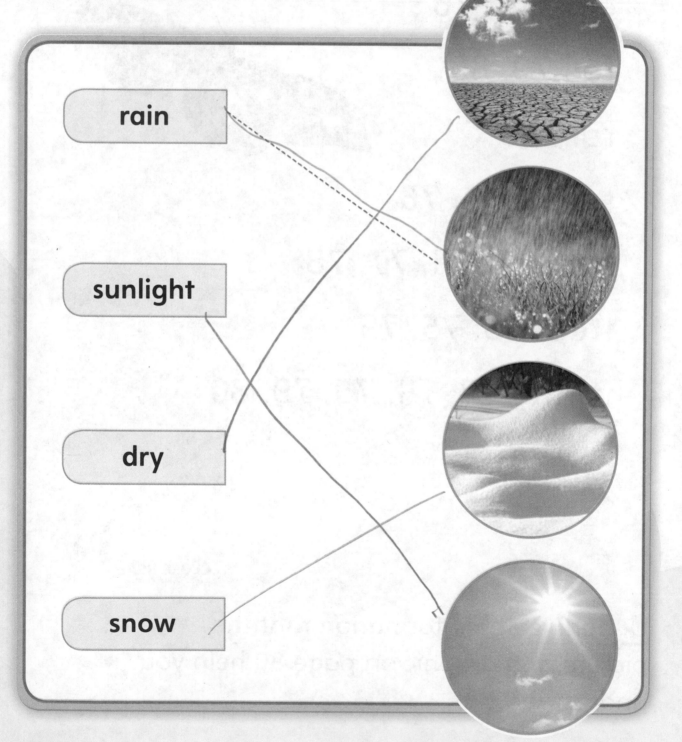

rain

sunlight

dry

snow

Check for Understanding

MY TURN Write the answers to the questions. You can look back at the text.

1. What makes this an informational text?

_____

_____

_____

_____

2. Why does the author use Did You Know? boxes?

_____

_____

_____

_____

3. What is the weather like near the equator? Use text evidence.

_____

_____

_____

_____

Use Text Features

Text features and graphics, such as photographs, help readers find and learn information. Photographs show more information about a topic.

MY TURN What information do you learn from the graphics? Go back to what you underlined in the text to help you answer.

_____

_____

_____

_____

_____

_____

_____

_____

_____

_____

TURN and TALK Talk about why the author uses graphics in this text.

Correct and Confirm Predictions

Readers can use text features to correct and confirm predictions they made before reading. Look at headings and other text features. Do they match what you predicted? If they match, you have confirmed your prediction. If they do not match, you need to correct your prediction.

MY TURN Think about the prediction you made before reading the text. How did the text features help you correct or confirm your prediction? Use what you highlighted to help you answer.

_____

_____

_____

_____

_____

_____

Reflect and Share

Write to Sources

You read about the seasons in different parts of the world. On a separate sheet of paper, write about in which part of the world you would like to live and why.

State an Opinion

When stating your opinion, you should:

• Share what you think or believe.

• Use text evidence to support your opinion.

Use the word **because** to show your reasons that support your opinion.

Weekly Question

What are seasons like around the world?

Read Together

I can make and use words to read and write informational text.

My Learning Goal

Academic Vocabulary

Antonyms are words that have opposite meanings.

MY TURN Circle the word that is an antonym for the underlined word or words.

1. I did not <u>expect</u> the surprise rainstorm that happened yesterday.

2. I prefer fiction books about the seasons instead of <u>informational</u> books.

3. I just finished writing about summer. Now I have my fall writing <u>in process</u>.

Read Like a Writer, Write for a Reader

Authors use graphic features, such as pictures and illustrations, to help readers learn more information.

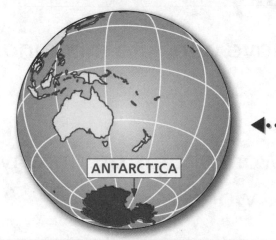

ANTARCTICA

The author uses the globe and label to show readers where the coldest place on Earth is.

This is the coldest place on Earth.

TURN and TALK Find another graphic feature in the text and talk about why the author uses it.

MY TURN Draw a graphic, or picture, to help readers learn more about summer.

Spell Long i Words

The letters **igh** spell the long **i** sound in **tight**.

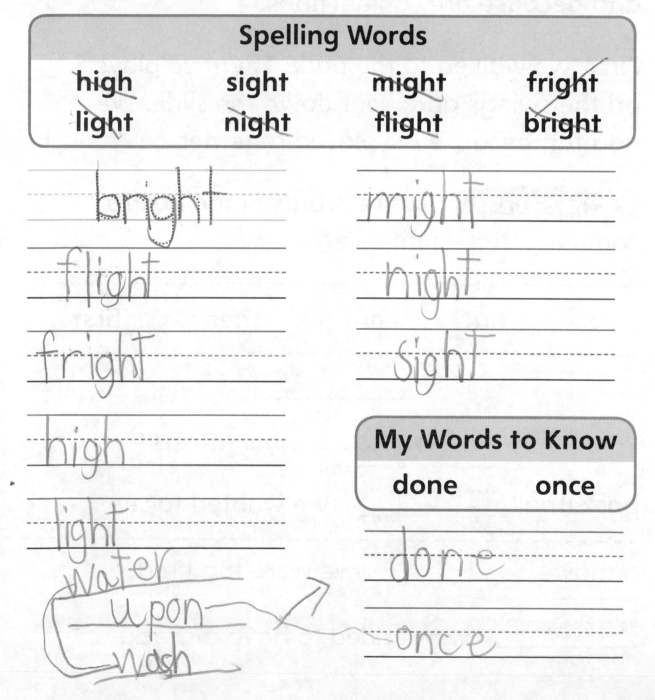 **MY TURN** Alphabetize each set of words.
Look at the first letter and then the second letter.

Spelling Words

high	sight	might	fright
light	night	flight	bright

bright

flight

fright

high

light

water
upon
wash

might

night

sight

My Words to Know

done   once

done

once

89

Transitions and Conjunctions

Transition words and **conjunctions** are used to connect two ideas. **First, next, then,** and **last** are transition words. **But, so, and, or,** and **because** are conjunctions.

First, we walked to the park. **Then** we played on the swings **and** went down the slide. We had fun **because** we played together.

MY TURN Use the words in the box to complete these sentences.

so	but	and	then	first

First _____ Lucy _____ I played basketball. _____ we wanted to see a movie, _____ we were too tired. _____ we decided to have a snack.

I can write a how-to book.

My Learning Goal

Compose an Introduction and a Conclusion

An **introduction** gets readers interested in the topic. A **conclusion** provides a sense of closure on the topic.

MY TURN Write an introduction and conclusion for the how-to topic.

Topic: How to Make a Bed

Introduction _____

_____

_____

Conclusion _____

_____

MY TURN Compose an introduction and conclusion for your how-to book.

Compose Instructions

Instructions are the directions on how to make or do something. Instructions include sentences that often begin with a verb. They use specific and relevant details to develop their ideas. That means the details are exact and on topic.

Plant the **sunflower** seed.
Water the soil **with enough water
so that the soil is wet.**

MY TURN Write instructions on how to brush your teeth. Use specific and relevant details.

_____

- -

_____

- -

_____

- -

_____

MY TURN Compose instructions for your how-to book. Use specific and relevant details.

Create Simple Graphics

How-to books use simple graphics to give more details about the instructions. **Simple graphics** are pictures or drawings that can have labels.

MY TURN Read the step. Then draw a simple graphic that adds details to the writing. Add a label.

1. Fill a bucket with water.

MY TURN Include simple graphics as you develop your draft for your how-to book.

Seasonal Activities

MY TURN When you interact with a text, you read and respond to it in a way that helps you understand it. Interact with this text by circling the name of a season.

Spring

People can plant flowers and watch them bloom.

Summer

People can cool off in the hot summer by swimming in a pool, lake, or ocean.

Autumn

Some people jump in the colorful leaves that fall off the trees.

What do people like about the seasons?

MY TURN Draw a picture of an activity you might do in the season you circled.

Winter

Many people go sledding, skiing, and snowboarding.

Segment and Blend Sounds

SEE and SAY Say each picture name. Then segment the words by saying each sound. Blend the sounds together as you say the picture names again.

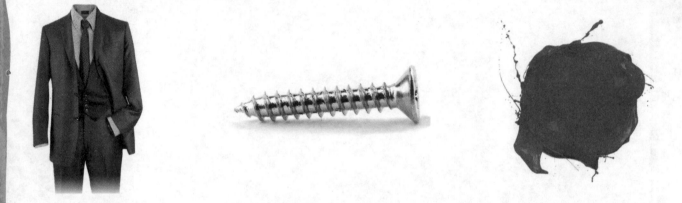

Vowel Teams ue, ew, ui

The letters **ue**, **ew**, and **ui** make the vowel sound in **blue**, **screw**, and **suit**.

MY TURN Read these words.

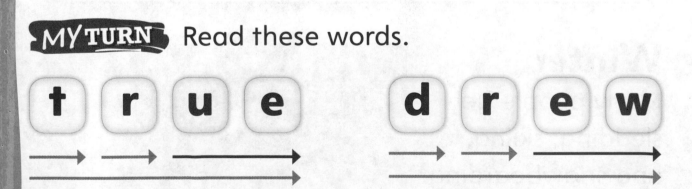

Vowel Teams ue, ew, ui

TURN and TALK Read these words.

true	**grew**	**cruise**
due	**chew**	**juice**
clue	**flew**	**fruit**

MY TURN Say each picture name.
Highlight the words that name the pictures.

suit   ring   box   screw   red   blue

Vowel Teams ue, ew, ui

MY TURN Use a word from the box to finish each sentence.

new	glue	juice

1. I help things stick together. I am ___glue___.

2. I am a sweet drink. I am _____.

3. We are not old. We are _____.

MY TURN Write a new sentence with one of the words you wrote.

_____

_____

_____

Segment and Blend Sounds

SEE and SAY To make words, we segment, or separate, sounds and then blend, or combine, them. Segment the sounds in each picture name. Then blend the sounds to say the picture name again.

Prefixes re-, un-

A **prefix** is a word part that is added to the beginning of a word to make a new word.

The prefix **re-** means "again."

The prefix **un-** means "not" or "the opposite of."

MY TURN Read these words.

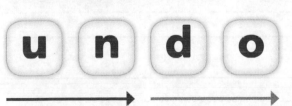

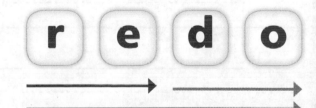

My Words to Know

Some words you must remember and practice.

MY TURN Read these words.

| off | open | laugh | because | sentence |

MY TURN Finish the sentences.

1. I take a book _____off_____ the shelf.

2. I _____ it and read a _____.

Handwriting Always print sentences clearly. Leave spaces between words.

MY TURN Print a sentence using a word you did not use. Leave spaces between the words.

_____

_____

_____

Prefixes re-, un-

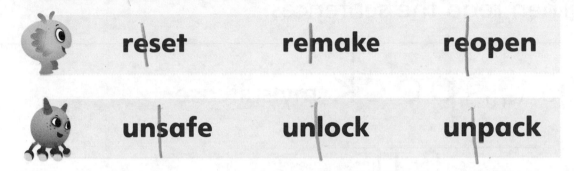 **TURN** *and* **TALK** Read these words.

reset	remake	reopen

unsafe	unlock	unpack

MY TURN Write the correct prefix to create a word that fits the definition.

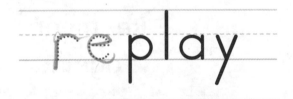

replay   play again

unseen   not seen

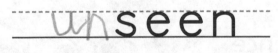

unzip   the opposite of **zip**

retry   try again

Prefixes re-, un-

MY TURN Write **un-** or **re-** to finish each word. Then read the sentences.

I have to _un_**pack** my suitcase.

Can you _re_**fill** the ice bucket?

I will _un_**lock** the door.

> **Un-** means "not."
> **Re-** means "again."

MY TURN Write a sentence using a word with the prefix **re-** or **un-**.

can atleast just unpack the backpack.

Best Time of the Year

Drew likes summer because of the hot sun and blue sky.

He can unzip his coat.

He can take off his hat.

AUDIO

Audio with Highlighting

ANNOTATE

Read the story. Highlight the two words that have the same vowel sound as **clue.**

103

<u>Unlike</u> Drew, Sue picks winter.

This sentence makes her laugh:

"It will snow ten inches!"

She unpacks her snowsuit.

<u>Underline</u> the two words with prefixes.

Newt likes spring because
that's when things regrow.
The fruit trees start to bud.
Then the buds start to open.

Highlight the two words that have
the same vowel sound as **clue.**

My Learning Goal

I can read about the seasons.

Persuasive Text

A persuasive text gives an opinion and reasons to persuade, or convince, readers to think something or do something.

Reading Is Fun!

Opinion ── I like to read. You should like to read too. It is fun to

Reasons ── read. You can learn new things. You can see pictures you like. We should all like to read.

TURN and TALK How is persuasive text different from informational text?

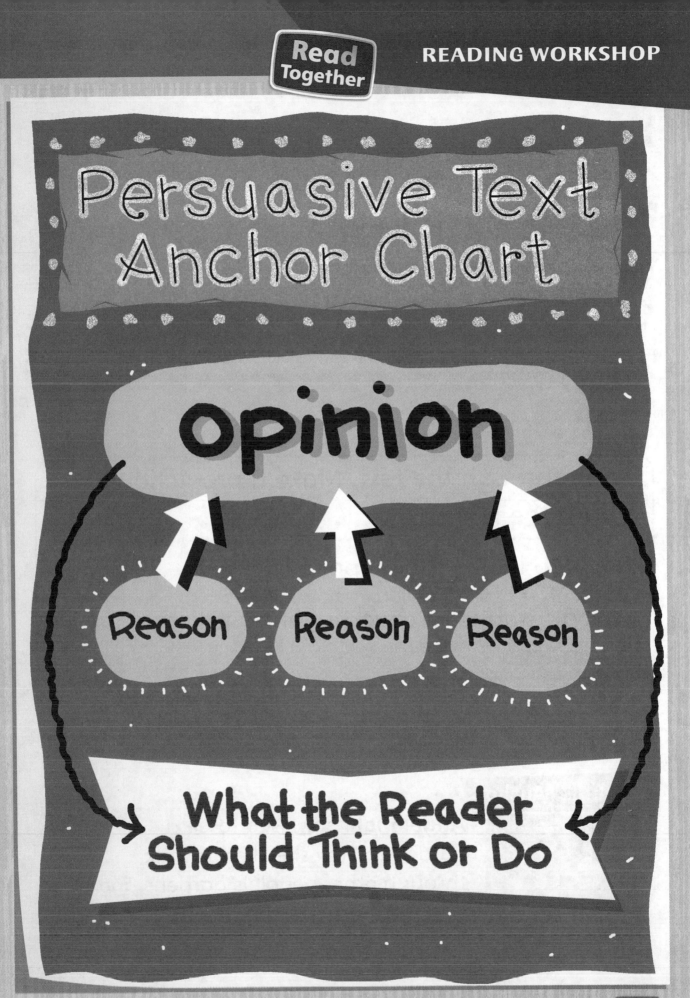

In Spring

Preview Vocabulary

You will read these words in *In Spring*.

| fawns | worms | squirrels |

Read

Look through the text. Make a prediction about the text.

Read to learn about spring.

Ask questions to check if your prediction is correct.

Talk about the author's opinion about spring.

Meet the Author

Angela Johnson used to be a gardener. Now she likes to walk through other people's gardens and think about her writing.

In Spring

written by Angela Johnson ❀ illustrated by Giovana Medeiros

AUDIO

Audio with Highlighting

ANNOTATE

Why is spring the best season?
There are so many reasons.
Just ask me!

In spring, days get warmer. You can feel <u>breezes</u> blow hints of hotter days. You can feel the sun's warmth on your <u>neck</u>.

CLOSE READ

Highlight the words that help you make a prediction about the text.

In spring, days get longer. You can run outside after dinner without a coat. You can watch squirrels dart around.

In spring, plants start growing again. You can walk in the woods and spy <u>flowers</u> hiding behind trees.

CLOSE READ

<u>Underline</u> the reasons the author gives to persuade readers that spring is the best season.

In spring, you can see worms coil up from underneath the wet ground. You can wear boots and splash through puddles.

In spring, animals have babies. You can see tadpoles swimming beneath the pond's melting ice. You can see fawns struggling to walk on their young legs.

CLOSE READ

<u>Underline</u> the reasons the author gives to persuade readers that spring is the best season.

Spring is the best season. It links the cold of winter with the heat of summer. It waves good-bye to one season and welcomes another.

There are so many reasons to like spring. Don't you think so too?

CLOSE READ

<u>Underline</u> what the author is trying to persuade readers to think.

Develop Vocabulary

MY TURN Draw a line from each word to the picture that shows its meaning.

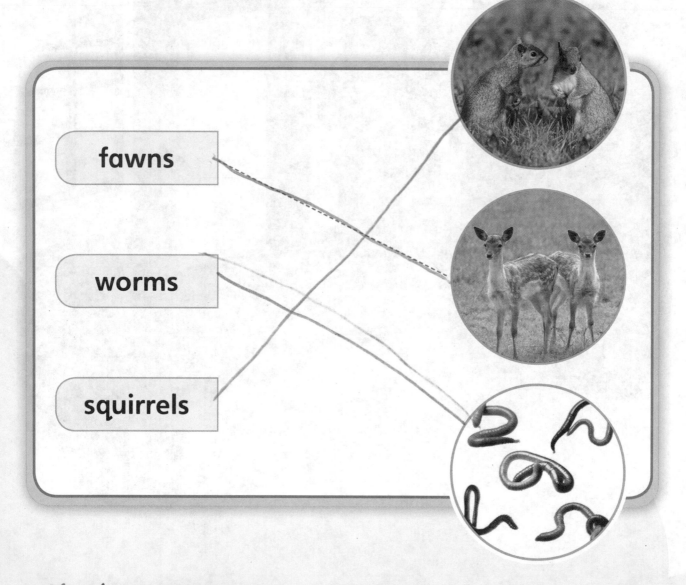

fawns

worms

squirrels

TURN and TALK Use the vocabulary words to talk about spring.

Check for Understanding

MY TURN Write the answers to the questions. You can look back at the text.

1. How can you tell this is a persuasive text?

_____

_____

_____

_____

2. Why does the author use words such as **dart** and **melting?**

_____

_____

_____

3. How are plants and animals similar in spring? Use text evidence.

_____

_____

Identify Persuasive Text

Persuasive text has opinions and reasons that try to convince readers to think something or do something.

MY TURN What is the author trying to persuade readers to think? Go back to what you underlined in the text to help you answer.

The author wants readers to think that

_____

_____

_____

_____

What is one reason the author uses?

_____

_____

_____

_____

_____

Correct and Confirm Predictions

During reading, readers can correct, or adjust, a prediction. After reading, they can confirm, or check, if their prediction was right. Looking at how text is organized, or text structure, will help you correct and confirm predictions. What is the text structure? Do you see an opinion and reasons?

MY TURN What did you predict about the text? Look back at what you highlighted.

I predicted this text would be about

_____

_____

because _____

_____

_____

Was my prediction correct? (Circle)   Yes   No

TURN and TALK Talk with your partner about how the structure helped you correct or confirm your prediction.

Reflect and Share

Write to Sources

You have read informational texts and a persuasive text about the seasons. On a separate sheet of paper, tell how the topics of these texts are similar and different.

Use Text Evidence

When comparing and contrasting two texts, it is important to:

- Use text evidence from both texts.
- Explain how the text evidence shows ways in which the texts are alike and different.

Weekly Question

What do people like about the seasons?

Read Together

My Learning Goal

I can make and use words to connect reading and writing.

Academic Vocabulary

Context clues are words or pictures that help you figure out what a word means.

MY TURN Read the sentences. Highlight the context clues that help you understand the meanings of the underlined words.

1. I <u>sensed</u> something. It was the wind that I felt.

2. I <u>expect</u> an early spring because I predict warmer weather is coming.

3. Some <u>informational</u> books can tell you facts about spring.

Read Like a Writer, Write for a Reader

Authors choose words that help readers visualize information in the text.

> You can see worms **coil up** . . .

◀········ The author uses these words to help readers picture what the worms are doing.

MY TURN Write about something else you see in spring. Use words that will help readers visualize your writing.

My
Learning
Goal

I can write a how-to book.

Organize with Structure

Authors organize the structure of their how-t books. They include an introduction, steps in order, and a conclusion.

MY TURN Organize the text. Circle the introduction. **Highlight** the steps. Underline the conclusion.

Soon your plant will start to grow!
I will show you how to grow a plant.
Plant a seed in a pot of soil. Then water the soil.
Next, place the pot in a sunny spot.

MY TURN Develop your how-to draft by organizing the structure.

Steps in a Process

Authors often use numbers to write the steps of their how-to books in order.

1. Buy a birdfeeder.

2. Pour seeds into the birdfeeder.

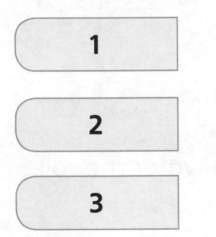**MY TURN** Draw a line to match each step to the correct number so that the steps are in order.

Planting a Seed

1	Place the seed in the hole.
2	Cover up the seed with soil.
3	Dig a small hole in the soil.

MY TURN Use numbered steps to develop your how-to book.

Features and Simple Graphics

How-to books have features and simple graphics that show readers how to follow steps or instructions. Simple graphics can be pictures or drawings.

MY TURN Read the steps. Draw a simple graphic that shows how to follow one of the steps.

1. Fill a watering pot with water.
2. Pour water over the flower.

MY TURN Add text features and simple graphics to one of your drafts.

Season to Season

In springtime, I smell the sweet air.

In summer, I feel the sun's glare.

In autumn, I hear the crisp leaves blow.

In winter, I see the falling snow.

How do we know when the seasons are changing?

MY TURN Interacting with a text means you read and respond to it in a way that helps you understand it. Interact with this poem by writing about a season using one of the five senses.

Remove Sounds

SEE and SAY Name the pictures. Remove, or take away, the first sound in each picture name. Then say the new words.

Long i, Long o

Words that end in **i** plus the consonant blend **ld** or **nd** often have the long **i** sound, as in **mild** or **mind**. Words that end in **o** plus the consonant blend **ld** or **st** often have the long **o** sound, as in **hold** or **host**.

MY TURN Read these words.

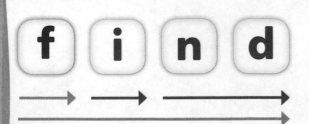 

Long i, Long o

TURN and TALK Read these words.

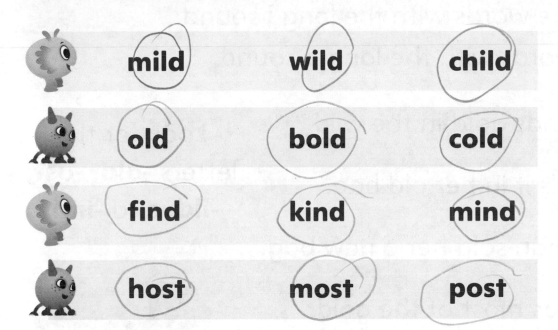

mild	wild	child
old	bold	cold
find	kind	mind
host	most	post

MY TURN Say each picture name. Write **i** or **o** to finish each word. Read the words.

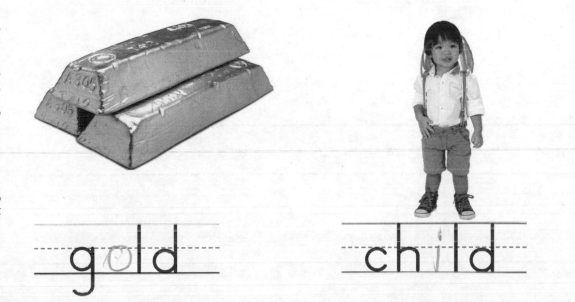

gold   child

Long i, Long o

MY TURN Read the sentences.
Underline words with the long **i** sound.
Circle words with the long **o** sound.

Sandy finds gold in the wild.

She holds it in her old bag.

A kind man sold her a new bag.

Sandy has most of the gold.

> Look for the letters **-old, -ost, -ild,** and **-ind.**

MY TURN Write a new
sentence about the gold.

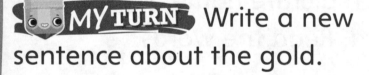

The gold

Segment and Blend Sounds

 **SEE and SAY** We blend, or combine, sounds to make words. Say each sound as you name each picture. Then blend the sounds to say the picture name again.

Suffixes -ly, -ful

A **suffix** is a word part added to the end of a word. It makes a new word.

The suffix **-ly** means **"in a __ way."**
The suffix **-ful** means **"full of __."**

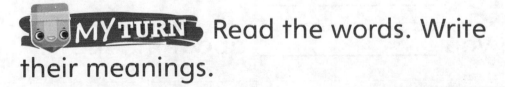 **MY TURN** Read the words. Write their meanings.

hopeful _____ hope

loudly _____ loud

My Words to Know

Some words you must identify and remember.

MY TURN Read these words.

move	only	learn	eight	house

MY TURN Write words from the box to complete the sentences. Read the sentences.

1. We can leave your house by _____.

2. We have to _____ before it snows.

3. When did you _____ about the snow?

4. I found out _____ last night.

Suffixes -ly, -ful

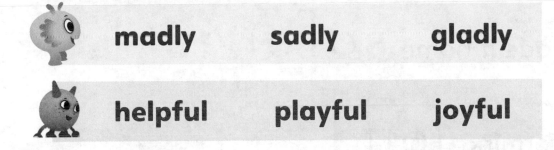 **TURN and TALK** Read these words.

madly	sadly	gladly
helpful	playful	joyful

MY TURN Write **-ly** or **-ful** to make a word that fits the definition.

sadly — in a sad way

skillful — full of skill

hopeful — full of hope

safely — in a safe way

Suffixes -ly, -ful

MY TURN Write the suffix **-ly** or **-ful** to finish the words. Then read each sentence.

1. We made it home safe**ly**.

2. It is storming loud**ly**.

3. I am hope**ful** that it will end soon.

MY TURN Write another sentence that includes a word with the suffix **-ly** or **-ful**.

Signs of Change

The sun beams brightly.

Ice melts from every house.

People are more cheerful.

No one minds the mild air.

AUDIO

Audio with Highlighting

ANNOTATE

Read the story. Highlight the two words with **suffixes**.

Most trees turn gold and red.

It's time to learn again!

Some are joyful as they enter.

Others move more slowly.

Fall

Underline the two words with the long **o** sound spelled **o**.

The wind blows wild and cold.

Eight inches of snow fall.

Only the bold go out in that.

How can they find their way?

Highlight the two words with the long i sound spelled i.

My Learning Goal   I can read about the seasons.

Fiction

Fiction is a made-up story with characters, setting, plot, and a theme. A theme is the message or big idea.

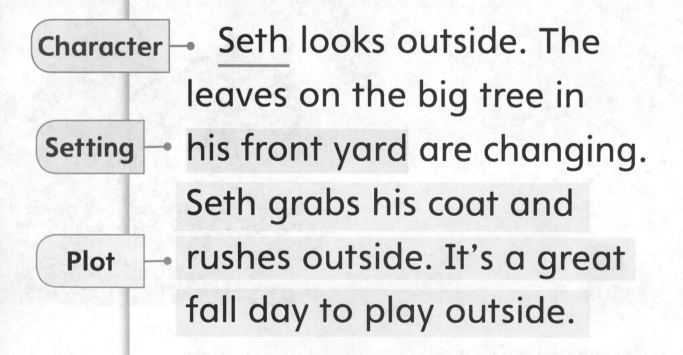

A Fall Day

Character ⟶ <u>Seth</u> looks outside. The leaves on the big tree in

Setting ⟶ his front yard are changing. Seth grabs his coat and

Plot ⟶ rushes outside. It's a great fall day to play outside.

TURN and TALK How is fiction different from informational text?

Fiction Anchor Chart

characters

setting

theme

plot

Fiction
made up by
the author

My Autumn Book

Preview Vocabulary

You will read these words in *My Autumn Book*.

crisp	chilly	breeze

Read

Think about the type of text. Make a prediction.

Read to learn about the theme.

Ask what ideas are most important.

Talk about what you found interesting.

Meet *the* Author

Wong Herbert Yee writes and illustrates picture books. His love for drawing started in first grade after his teacher pinned one of his drawings to the class bulletin board.

My Autumn Book

written by
Wong Herbert Yee

AUDIO

Audio with Highlighting

ANNOTATE

The air is crisp.

The sky turns gray.

Is autumn really on the way?

Downstairs I rush.

I can hardly wait,

To go outside and investigate.

In a corner of the garden shed,

Spider spins a silken thread.

Hello, Spider!

What are you weaving?

Is it true that summer

Is leaving?

Crickets chirruping in the clover ...

Another sign that warm days are over.

CLOSE READ

<u>Underline</u> the words that tell the topic, or what the text is about.

A chilly wind blows. I zip my jacket.

From the treetops I hear a racket.

The buzzing gets louder. It fills the air.

Cicada is warning us: Better beware!

Summer is leaving! Autumn coming!

Woodpecker agrees, *rap-a-tap* drumming.

Chipmunk scampers past,

Seeds packed in its cheeks,

Finding food for the upcoming weeks.

Squirrel digs a hole to bury its treasure.

Squirrel is expecting a change in the weather.

CLOSE READ

Highlight the details that tell autumn is coming.

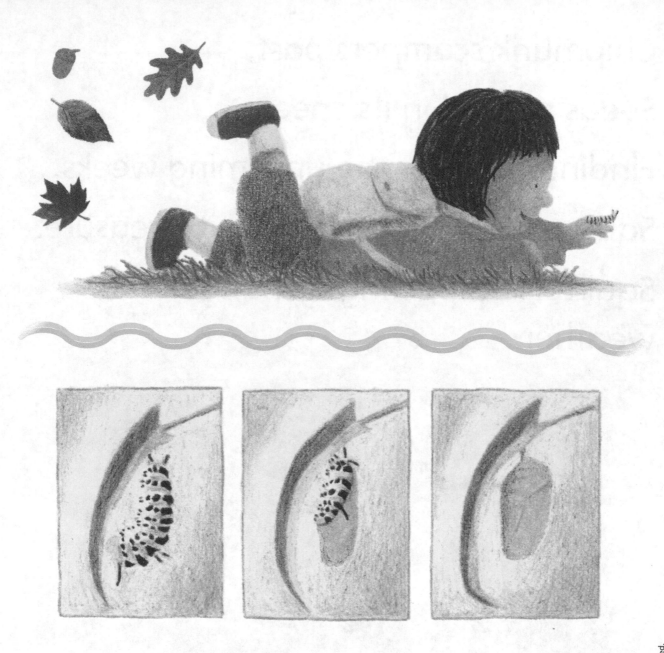

Caterpillar knows it's time to cocoon.

Ker-YAK! Blue Jay cries.

Autumn so soon?

Geese honk above,

Fly south in formation.

Trees dressing up for the fall celebration.

VOCABULARY IN CONTEXT

Context clues are words and pictures that help readers figure out what a new word means. What does the word **cocoon** mean? What part of the picture helps you figure that out?

151

Dogwood shows off
A new crimson gown.

Oak changes into
A suit of rust brown.

Ash cloaked in yellow.

Maple wears red.

Aspen, a crown of gold
on its head.

Together they whisper and sway
in the breeze,

Shaking loose acorns and batches
of leaves.

Swirling and twirling, leaves spinning
round,

A whirlwind of color that blankets
the ground.

CLOSE READ

Highlight the words that describe what
happens to the trees' leaves. Use the
pictures to help you.

I search high and low,

Find one of each—

A ginkgo, a willow,

An elm, birch, and beech.

Summer is leaving, fall's on its way.

The seasons are changing,

No time to delay.

I dash up to my room

And open the door.

Empty my pack,

Spread things on the floor.

I find a jar for the acorns ...

Fetch scissors and glue—

A pad of paper,

And crayons, too.

I decorate pages,

Arrange to make space ...

There, it's all done!

Everything is in place.

CLOSE READ

<u>Underline</u> the text that helps you figure out the theme, or big idea.

When crickets no longer sing late at night

And the world outside

Has turned cold, black and white ...

... I'll lie by the fire

With my book and remember,

Until autumn returns

Once more in September.

CLOSE READ

Highlight the details that tell winter
is here.

159

Develop Vocabulary

MY TURN Use the words from the box to complete the sentences about autumn.

crisp	chilly	breeze

1. The air feels crisp.

2. Can you feel the _____?

3. A _____ wind makes me shiver.

Check for Understanding

MY TURN Write the answer to each question. You can look back at the text.

1. What makes the text fiction?

_____

_____

_____

_____

2. Find an adjective the author uses. Why does he use this word?

_____

_____

_____

_____

3. How are the animals and trees similar? Use text evidence.

_____

_____

_____

_____

Determine Theme

A **theme** is the central message, or big idea, of a text. Details and your own experiences can help you determine the theme.

MY TURN Draw a picture of the theme of *My Autumn Book*. Use what you underlined in the text to help you determine the theme.

MY TURN Write about the theme.

_____

- -

_____

_____

- -

_____

Find Important Details

Details are the important pieces of information in a text. Details can help you figure out the theme.

MY TURN Draw an important detail that tells about the theme. Look back at what you highlighted in the text.

TURN and TALK How do the details relate to the topic and theme of the text?

Reflect and Share

Talk About It

Retell *My Autumn Book*. How is the theme of *My Autumn Book* similar to themes in other texts you have read?

Retell a Text

When retelling a text, you should:

- Tell the important events in your own words.
- Use important details from the text.

Use the words on the note to help you retell the text.

In the beginning . . .

Now retell the text.

Weekly Question

How do we know when the seasons are changing?

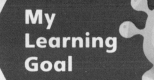

I can make and use words to connect reading and writing.

My Learning Goal

Academic Vocabulary

Word parts can be added to some words to make new words with different meanings.

MY TURN Read the words. Use a word from the box to complete the sentences.

sensible	unexpected

1. The weather quickly changed.

   _____

   It was _____ .

2. It was chilly, so Jenny grabbed her jacket.

   _____

   She is _____ .

Read Like a Writer, Write for a Reader

Authors choose words that make readers use their senses. The words help readers visualize, or imagine, how things feel, sound, taste, smell, and look.

The **buzzing** gets louder.
It fills the air.

◄········ The author uses these words to help readers imagine what the buzzing sounds like.

TURN and TALK Talk about other words the author uses in the text to help readers visualize.

MY TURN Write sentences about the weather. The words should help you use your senses.

_____

_____

_____

_____

I can write a how-to book.

My Learning Goal

Edit for Prepositions

Authors use **prepositions** to tell how a noun or pronoun is related to words in other parts of the sentence.

You need to spread the materials **on the floor.**

MY TURN Edit the sentences by replacing the underlined word with a preposition from the box.

on	for	below

1. Grab the leaves <u>after</u> the tree. _below_

2. Find a jar <u>in</u> the leaves. _____

3. Draw the leaves <u>off</u> the pages. _____

MY TURN Edit your how-to book for prepositions.

Edit for Adverbs That Convey Time

Authors use adverbs to tell about a verb. Adverbs can tell when something happens.

The leaves will be changing **soon.** (tells when)

MY TURN Edit the sentences by adding an adverb that conveys time from the box.

| early | always | tomorrow | sometimes |

We will help rake the leaves tomorrow.

Mom thinks autumn came _____.

_____ we jump in the pile!

We _____have fun with Mom.

MY TURN Edit your how-to book for adverbs that convey time.

Edit for Punctuation Marks

Punctuation marks show where a sentence ends. Authors check that every sentence has a punctuation mark.

Declarative sentences end with periods. Interrogative sentences end with question marks. Exclamatory sentences end with exclamation marks.

MY TURN Edit the punctuation marks in the draft.

Do you see that _?_ The caterpillar is changing _!_

I can't believe it can make a cocoon _!_ What will

happen next _?_ Let's look it up in a book _._

MY TURN Edit the punctuation marks in your how-to book.

Animals in Winter

Migrate

Some animals move to a warm place. **Monarch butterflies** fly from Canada Mexico each —that is 3,000 miles!

Canada

U.S.A.

Mexico

Hibernate

Certain animals hibernate, or sleep through winter. This **painted turtle** will bury itself in mud and stay there all winter.

What do living things do in the winter?

Change

Some animals' bodies change to survive through the winter. **American bison** grow thick fur for warmth.

TURN and TALK Talk about which animal in winter is most interesting to you.

Read Together

Segment and Blend Sounds

SEE and SAY Say each sound as you name the pictures. Then say the words again.

Open and Closed Syllables

An **open syllable** ends in a vowel.
It usually has a long vowel sound.
A **closed syllable** is closed off by a consonant.
The vowel sound is usually short.
A word with one consonant between two vowels
can be divided into syllables before or after
the consonant.

MY TURN Read the words.

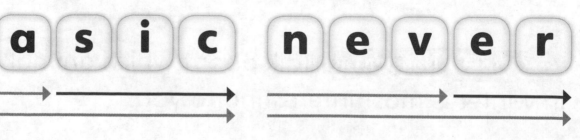

Open and Closed Syllables

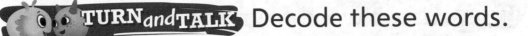 **TURN and TALK** Decode these words.

| silent | music | frozen |

| limit | lemon | travel |

MY TURN Read each picture name. Draw a line to divide each word into syllables.

pilot

wagon

seven

tiger

Open and Closed Syllables

MY TURN Use a word from the box to finish each sentence. Then read the sentences.

silent	spider	shadow

Robin makes a shadow on the wall.

Her arms make the shape of a _____.

Robin has fun with this _____ game!

MY TURN Write your own sentence using one of the words from the box.

_____

_____

_____

_____

Manipulate Sounds

 **SEE and SAY** Say each sound as you name the pictures. Then manipulate the sounds to make a new word. When you manipulate the sounds, you switch them around in a new order.

Vowel Teams oo, ou

The letters **oo** and **ou** can make the vowel sound you hear in **moon**.

MY TURN Read these words.

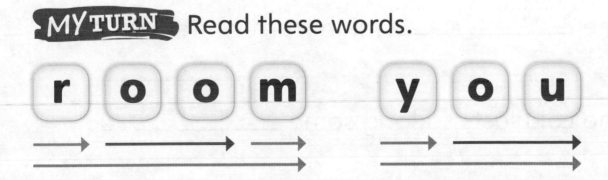

My Words to Know

Some words you must remember and practice.

MY TURN Read these words.

| warm | today | world | years | should |

MY TURN Complete each sentence with a word from the box. Read the sentences.

1. _Today_ is a _____ fall day.

2. But it _____ turn cold soon.

3. The _____ might turn white with snow.

4. The cold lasts so long some _____.

Vowel Teams oo, ou

TURN and TALK Read these words.

zoo   moose   tooth

you   soup   group

MY TURN Say each picture name.
Underline the word that names each picture.

boot   bat   <u>pool</u>   poll

stop   <u>soup</u>   <u>moon</u>   man

Vowel Teams oo, ou

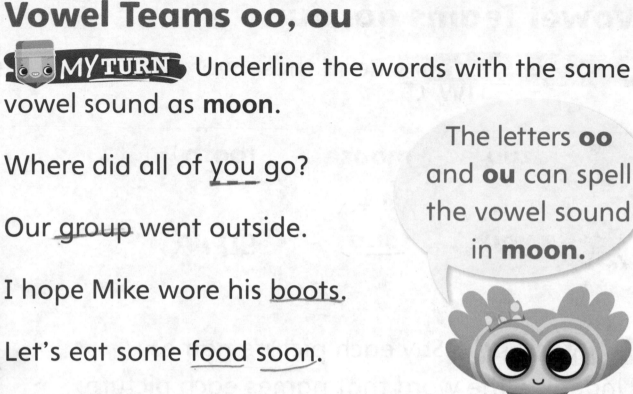

MY TURN Underline the words with the same vowel sound as **moon**.

Where did all of <u>you</u> go?

Our <u>group</u> went outside.

I hope Mike wore his <u>boots</u>.

Let's eat some <u>food</u> <u>soon</u>.

The letters **oo** and **ou** can spell the vowel sound in **moon**.

MY TURN Write sentences with **oo** and **ou** words.

The moon is far away.

The soup is hot.

In Winter

We saw geese fly over us.

The group flew in a V shape.

They travel to locate food and a <u>warm</u> place for the winter.

AUDIO

Audio with Highlighting

ANNOTATE

Read the story. Highlight the three two-syllable words that begin with a closed syllable.

Should moose leave too?

Their world is <u>frozen</u> solid.

So, bark is their major food.

<u>Underline</u> the two two-syllable words that begin with an open syllable.

Today we stay warm in
our cabin.

We sip hot soup
with spoons.

We put on boots and coats.

It feels like years until spring.

<u>Underline</u> the three words with the
same vowel sound as **moon**.

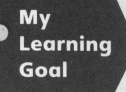

My Learning Goal

I can read informational text.

SPOTLIGHT ON GENRE

Informational Text

An informational text often uses graphics, or pictures, to add details or show information in a visual way.

Squirrels gather food to prepare for winter.

Be a Fluent Reader Fluent readers read with accuracy. That means they read every word without any mistakes. It takes practice to read accurately. After you read this week's text, practice reading accurately with a partner.

Informational Text Anchor Chart

Words and Pictures

Many birds fly south for the winter

Words and pictures work together to help readers understand a topic.

Signs of Winter

Preview Vocabulary

You will read these words in *Signs of Winter*.

| seasons | weather | daylight | temperature |

Read

Read to learn the big idea in this text.

Look at the photos to help you understand the text.

Ask questions about confusing parts.

Talk about how the illustrations and text work together.

Meet the Author

Colleen Dolphin writes children's books about science and math topics. She also wrote books about the signs of autumn, spring, and summer.

AUDIO

Audio with Highlighting

ANNOTATE

SIGNS OF Winter

written by

Colleen Dolphin

Seasons

Winter

Spring

There are four seasons during the year. They are called spring, summer, autumn, and winter. The weather, plants, animals, and daylight hours **change** during each season.

Summer

Autumn

Winter

Did You Know?

In France it is winter in December. In New Zealand it is winter in July.

During the year, Earth travels around the sun. This brings some parts of Earth closer to the sun. Other parts of Earth get farther from the sun. Winter happens in the parts farthest from the sun.

CLOSE READ

Underline what can change during each season.

In the winter, there are many clouds in the sky. Instead of raining, it snows. Vanessa and Tom are building a snowman. They start by making a huge snowball.

There is very little daylight in winter. It gets <u>dark</u> out early in the evening.

CLOSE READ

Look at the <u>text and illustrations</u> on these two pages. <u>Underline</u> the words that describe what you see in each illustration.

Did You Know?

Pine and fir trees have **needles**. The needles stay on the trees during winter.

In winter many trees are bare. Their branches don't have any leaves.

The **temperature** can get very cold during the winter. People need to wear extra clothes to keep warm. James is making a snow angel. His coat and snow pants keep him from getting cold.

VOCABULARY IN CONTEXT

Context clues are words or pictures that help you figure out what an unknown word means. Underline the words that help you figure out what the word **bare** means. Use the picture too.

Did You Know?

An American bison's coat grows extra long and thick in the winter.

The **temperature** is cold for animals too. Some move to warmer places for the winter. Animals that have a lot of fur stay during the winter. Their fur keeps them warm.

It is hard for animals to find food in the winter. In autumn, beavers **collect** extra sticks and logs. They keep them in the water near their lodges. They eat the bark during the winter.

Did You Know?
Winter comes after autumn and before spring.

CLOSE READ

What inference can you make about what bison do in cold temperatures? Highlight the text that helped you.

Bobby likes to go **sledding** in the winter. What do you do in the winter?

Glossary

change—to be altered or become different.

collect—to pick up or gather things from different places.

needle—a thin, pointy leaf on a pine or fir tree.

sled—a wooden or plastic vehicle that you sit on to ride down a snowy hill. Doing this is called sledding.

temperature—a measure of how hot or cold something is.

FLUENCY

Read pages 192 and 193 aloud with a partner to practice reading accurately.

Develop Vocabulary

MY TURN Read the word in each box. Then draw a picture that helps you remember what each word means.

seasons	weather
daylight	**temperature**

TURN and TALK Talk about what each vocabulary word means.

Check for Understanding

MY TURN Write the answers to the questions. You can look back at the text.

1. How do the photos help you know this text is an informational text?

_____

_____

_____

2. Why does the author write about people and animals in winter?

_____

_____

_____

3. What are signs of winter? Use text evidence.

_____

_____

_____

Use Pictures and Text

The pictures and words in a text give information about the topic. Both the pictures and words describe the key ideas in a text.

MY TURN Read the questions. Circle if you find the answer in the pictures, words, or both. Look back at what you underlined in the text.

How much daylight is in winter?	Picture	Words	Both
How can trees change during the seasons?	Picture	Words	Both

TURN and TALK Use the pictures and words to describe the key ideas in *Signs of Winter*.

Make Inferences

Readers make inferences. They use what they know and what they read to figure out something about the text.

MY TURN Make an inference about bison in *Signs of Winter*. Go back to what you highlighted in the text.

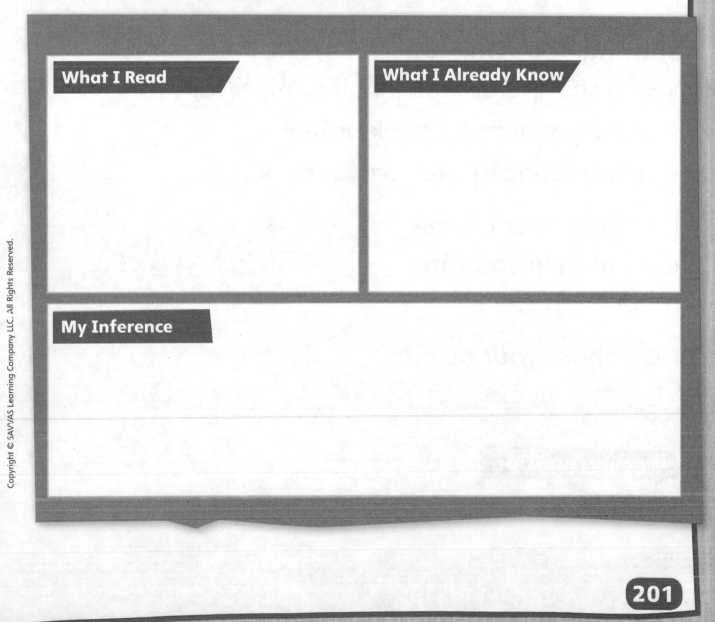

What I Read

What I Already Know

My Inference

Reflect and Share

Talk About It

You just read a text about winter. You also read other texts about the seasons. What is your opinion of winter? Use text evidence.

Sharing Your Opinion

When sharing an opinion, it is important to:

- Express what you think or feel.

- Use reasons to support your opinion.

Use the words on the note to help you form an opinion.

I think . . .
because . . .

Now share your opinion.

Weekly Question

What do living things do in the winter?

Read Together

I can make and use words to read and write informational text.

My Learning Goal

Academic Vocabulary

TURN and TALK Read the sentence starters. Finish the sentences together.

1. Some <u>information</u> I learned about seasons is . . .

2. My <u>sense</u> of smell is important because . . .

3. When it is summer, I <u>expect</u> to . . .

4. A <u>process</u> I know about is . . .

Read Like a Writer, Write for a Reader

Authors use graphics, or pictures, to help readers understand the topic.

An American bison's coat grows **extra long** and **thick** in the winter.

> The author chose the picture to help readers understand what the bison's coat looks like.

 TURN *and* **TALK** Find another graphic in the text and talk about why the author uses it.

MY TURN Draw a picture that will help readers understand this sentence.

Butterflies fly to warm places.

Spell Words with Open and Closed Syllables

The end of an **open syllable** is spelled with a vowel. The end of a **closed syllable** is spelled with a consonant.

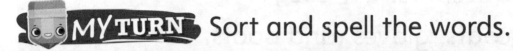 **MY TURN** Sort and spell the words.

Closed Syllable

cabin

Open Syllable

Spelling Words

robot

cabin

melon

begin

label

topic

seven

hotel

My Words to Know

My Words to Know

today

should

205

Commas in Dates and Sentences

A **comma** is a punctuation mark that is used to separate parts of sentences, parts of dates, and parts of a series, or list.

Monday, December 21, 2020
We need coats, gloves, and boots.

MY TURN Edit the sentences by adding commas.

Yesterday was Saturday, January 2 2021. We built snowmen went sledding and made snowballs. Tomorrow I hope we ice skate play hockey and make snow angels.

I can write a how-to book.

Edit for Spelling

Authors edit, or fix, spelling in their writing. They use spelling patterns and rules to check that words are spelled correctly. They need to remember how to spell other words.

I am **sevven** years old! seven

MY TURN Edit for spelling. Underline the misspelled words. Write the words correctly.

1. It is hot tooday. today

2. We can plaiy games outside. _____

3. Should we put on a cooat? _____

MY TURN Use spelling patterns and rules to edit for spelling in your how-to book.

Edit for Prepositions

Authors use a **preposition** to show how the noun that it follows is related to words in other parts of the sentence.

I wear gloves **in** winter.

MY TURN Read the sentences. Edit by writing the correct prepositions for the crossed-out word.

I am scared ~~from~~ spiders.   _of_

They arrived ~~to~~ school early.   _____

We live ~~in~~ Washington Street.   _____

My birthday is ~~on~~ July.   _____

MY TURN Edit the prepositions in your how-to book draft.

Publish and Celebrate

Publish your writing by making a final copy with no mistakes.

Celebrate your writing by sharing it with others. Use speaking and listening skills.

Celebrate Your Writing!

- Introduce yourself as the author by telling your name.
- Relate, or tell about, your experience writing.
- Express what you needed while writing.
- Express how you feel about your writing.

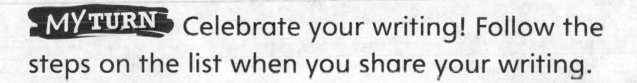 **MY TURN** Celebrate your writing! Follow the steps on the list when you share your writing.

UNIT THEME

Beyond My World

In Spring

_____

109

_____

Look back at each text.
Find a word or phrase
that describes a season.
Write the word or phrase.

WEEK 3

⭐ BOOK CLUB

WEEK 2

Seasons Around the World

_____

79

_____

⭐ BOOK CLUB

WEEK 1

Every Season

_____

27

_____

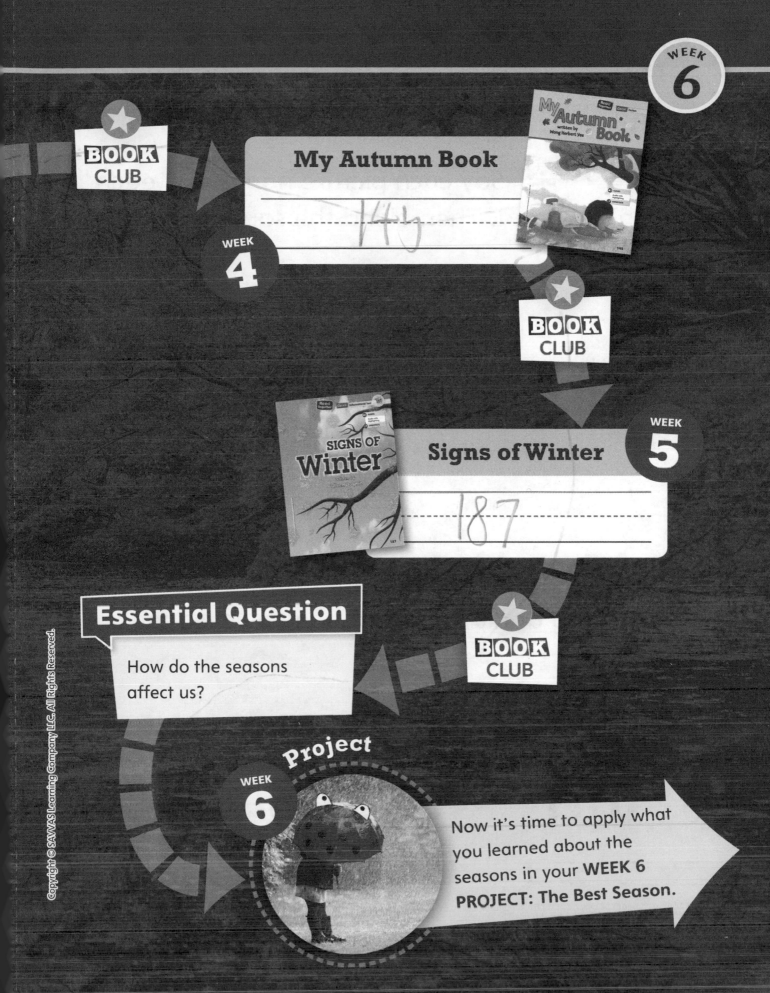

BOOK CLUB

My Autumn Book

WEEK 4

My Autumn Book
written by
Wong Herbert Yee

BOOK CLUB

SIGNS OF Winter

Signs of Winter

WEEK 5

187

BOOK CLUB

Essential Question

How do the seasons affect us?

Project

WEEK 6

Now it's time to apply what you learned about the seasons in your **WEEK 6 PROJECT: The Best Season.**

Segment and Blend Sounds

SEE and SAY Say each picture name. Say each sound in the word. Then blend the sounds to say the word.

Vowel Sound in foot

The letters **oo** and **u** can make the vowel sound in **foot**.

MY TURN Read these words.

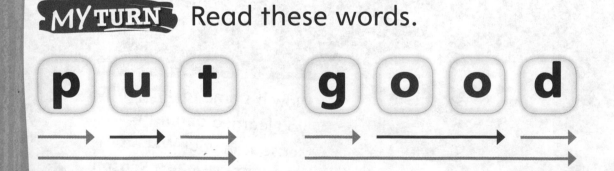

Vowel Sound in foot

 **TURN and TALK** Read these words.

took	**cook**	**look**

full	**pull**	**bull**

MY TURN Say each picture name. Circle the word that names the picture.

book back   bull ball

bash bush   hook hot

Vowel Sound in foot

MY TURN Read the sentences. Highlight words with the same vowel sound as **foot.**

Butch is my pet bull.

He can pull rocks from the brook.

He can push wood logs.

Butch sleeps in a nook in the barn.

The letters **oo** or **u** can make the vowel sound you hear in **foot.**

MY TURN Write a new sentence about Butch the bull.

Butch the bull

My Words to Know

Some words you must remember and practice.

MY TURN Read these words.

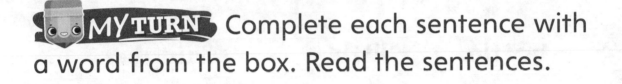

| mother | father | picture | another | through |

MY TURN Complete each sentence with a word from the box. Read the sentences.

1. My mother and _____ will go on a walk.

2. They want to walk _____ the woods.

3. They will pose for a _____.

4. Then they can go on _____ walk.

Final Syllable -le

TURN and TALK Read the words.

handle	middle	puzzle
gentle	simple	purple
bottle	little	struggle

MY TURN Write the letters **-le** to complete each word. Then read the words.

apple

beet

nood

bubb

Final Syllable -le

 **MY TURN** Draw a line to divide the words into syllables.

rat|tle   sample

paddle   wiggle

giggle   jungle

MY TURN Write a sentence using a word with the final syllable **-le.**

_____
- -
_____
_____
- -
_____
_____
- -
_____

Spring Rain

AUDIO

Audio with Highlighting

ANNOTATE

<u>Woody</u> put on his raincoat.

He pulled on his rain boots.

Look at that huge puddle!

He walked through
the middle.

Read the story. <u>Underline</u> the four
words with the same vowel sound
as **book.**

His mother laughed a little.

His father took a picture.

Woody saw another
big puddle.

With a giggle, he jumped in it.

Highlight the three words with the
final syllable **-le.**

His beagle <u>Butch</u> joins Woody.

They like a gentle spring rain.

It is good for the plants.

It is also a lot of fun. Splash!

<u>Underline</u> the three words with the same vowel sound as **book.**

The Best Season

Activity

Choose a season of the year. Write and perform a short play to persuade an audience that this season is the best.

RESEARCH

Let's Read!

This week you will read three articles about seasons.

1 **Summer and Winter Sports**

2 **Happy in Hawaii**

3 **Shine On, Sunshine!**

COLLABORATE With a partner, talk about which season is the best. Ask two questions for research.

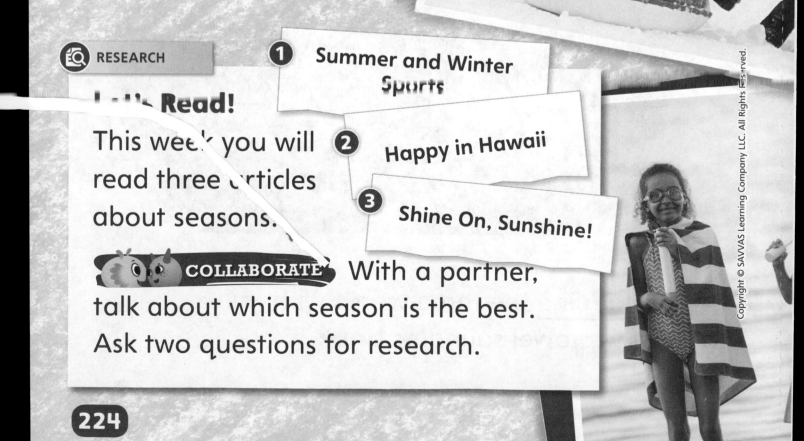

Use Academic Words

COLLABORATE Talk about the pictures with your partner. Respond using the academic words.

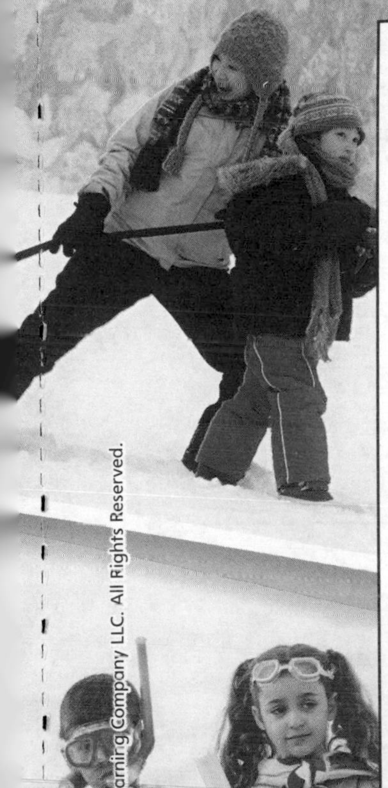

COLLABORATE With a partner, develop, or make, a research plan.

Best Season Research Plan

☐ Ask questions.

☐ _____

☐ _____

☐ _____

☐ _____

Power to Persuade

Sometimes authors write to persuade, or convince, readers to think or do something.

COLLABORATE Read "Happy in Hawaii" with a partner. Write your responses.

The author wants me to _____

_____

_____

One reason why the author would rather live in

Hawaii is _____

_____

_____

Did the author persuade you?   ☐ Yes   ☐ No

Search Online

🔍 **RESEARCH**

A **relevant source** has information that will help you answer questions. A Web site is one kind of source. You can use key words and phrases to search for relevant Web sites. Then you can gather, or collect, a list of Web sites you will use in your research.

My season is _____

One question about my season is

1. _____

COLLABORATE Write key words and phrases you will use to find and gather relevant sources.

_____

_____

Persuasive Play

A persuasive play can use characters and dialogue to persuade the audience to think or do something.

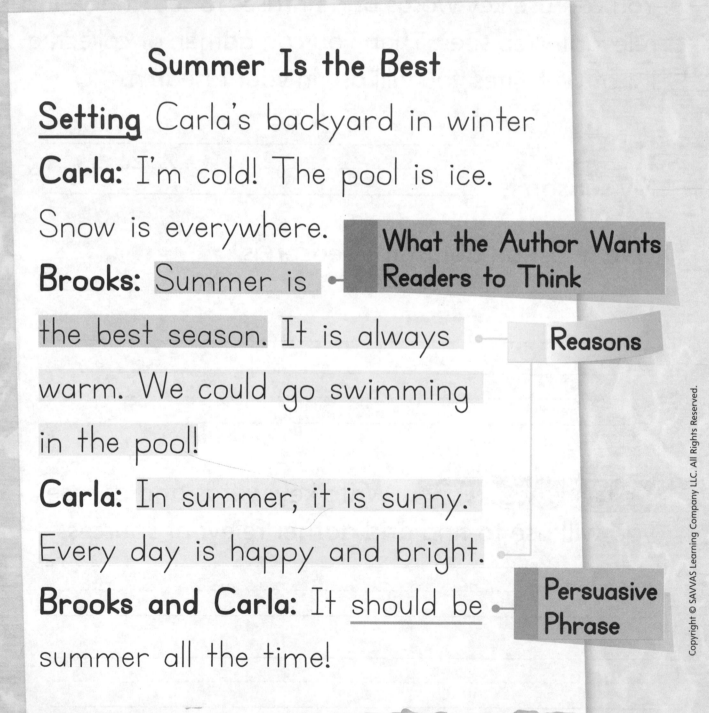

Summer Is the Best

Setting Carla's backyard in winter

Carla: I'm cold! The pool is ice. Snow is everywhere.

Brooks: Summer is the best season. It is always warm. We could go swimming in the pool!

Carla: In summer, it is sunny. Every day is happy and bright.

Brooks and Carla: It should be summer all the time!

What the Author Wants Readers to Think

Reasons

Persuasive Phrase

Just the Facts

When you identify and gather information, you find facts that answer your questions.

COLLABORATE Gather three facts about your season from your relevant sources.

1. _____

2. _____

3. _____

COLLABORATE Discuss how your facts answer your questions.

Set the Stage

Props, costumes, and visuals can help make your play more enjoyable for an audience.

costume

visual

prop

COLLABORATE With a partner, talk about props, costumes, and visuals you can use to perform your play.

Revise

 COLLABORATE Read your play with a partner.

> **Did you check your**
>
> opinion?　　　　yes　　　　no
>
> reasons?　　　　yes　　　　no
>
> persuasive
> words?　　　　　yes　　　　no

Does your opinion persuade readers to think your season is best?

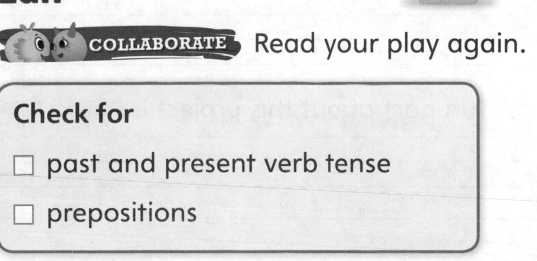

Edit

COLLABORATE Read your play again.

> **Check for**
>
> ☐ past and present verb tense
>
> ☐ prepositions

Share

COLLABORATE   Share your play.

- Perform your play using props, costumes, and visuals.

- Read your play aloud.

- Make a final copy for others to read.

Reflect

MY TURN   Complete the sentences.

One thing I like about my play is

_____
- -
_____
- -
_____

The most fun part about this project is

_____
- -
_____
- -
_____

Reflect on Your Goals

Look back at your unit goals. Use a different color to rate yourself again.

MY TURN Complete the sentences.

Reflect on Your Reading

My favorite text from this unit is

_____

_____

_____

Reflect on Your Writing

My favorite writing from this unit is

_____

_____

_____

----

because _____

_____

A strong opinion gives reasons for your thoughts.

I can write an opinion book.

Opinion Writing

An opinion tells what you think about something. Opinion books have:

- a topic
- an opinion
- reasons
- a conclusion

Opinion Writing Sandwich

Topic and Opinion

My favorite _____ is _____.

_____ is the best _____.

I like. . . I think. . .

I feel. . . I believe. . .

Reason

because

Conclusion

These are the reasons why. . .

Now you know why. . .

That explains why. . .

That is why. . .

Brainstorm Ideas

The topic of an opinion book should be something the author cares about. The author should have a strong opinion or feeling about the topic.

MY TURN What topics are interesting to you? List some of those topics. Circle the topic you will write about.

_____

_____

_____

_____

MY TURN What choices belong in that topic? List some of those. Circle the one you like the best.

_____

_____

_____

Plan Your Opinion Writing

MY TURN Plan your opinion book by writing down your ideas.

Topic

Opinion

Reason

Reason

My Learning Goal

I can write an opinion book.

Introduce a Topic

Authors introduce the topic by telling readers what they are writing about and clearly stating their opinion.

MY TURN Read the sentence below. Underline the words that tell the topic of the opinion piece.

I want to get the best pet.

MY TURN Write a sentence that tells the topic.

_____

_____

_____

_____

State an Opinion

An author clearly states, or tells, the opinion.

MY TURN Read the text. Underline the opinion.

> Not all animals make good pets. I think a fish would be a great pet.

MY TURN Write a sentence that tells your opinion about your topic.

_____

_____

_____

_____

_____

_____

Supply Reasons

An author gives reasons that support and explain the opinion.

MY TURN Write a sentence that tells a reason for the opinion.

A shark would be a bad pet.

_____

- -

_____

- -

_____

- -

_____

MY TURN In your opinion book, supply at least two reasons that support your opinion.

I can write an opinion book.

Organize Parts of the Page

Authors organize their opinion books before they write. They include the topic, opinion, reasons, and an ending.

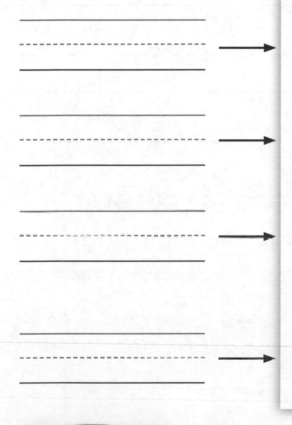 **MY TURN** Label each part.

We are trying to find the best pet for my family.

I think the best pet would be a fish.

It would be the best pet because it is quiet. It also can stay in my bedroom.

Those are a few reasons why I think a fish is a great pet.

MY TURN Develop your opinion book by organizing the parts of the page.

Organize Introduction

The **introduction** should include the topic and your opinion.

 MY TURN Write a sentence that introduces the topic of the best pet. Write a sentence that states what you think would be the best pet.

_____

- -

_____

- -

_____

- -

_____

MY TURN Draft an introduction to your own opinion book. Be sure to include the topic and your opinion.

Write a Conclusion

The **conclusion** ends an opinion book by reminding the reader of the author's opinion.

MY TURN Read the text. Write a sentence that would be a good conclusion.

> I think a parrot is the most interesting wild animal. Parrots are interesting because they can make many different sounds. Some parrots can live longer than a person.

_____

- -

_____

- -

_____

- -

_____

MY TURN Revise your opinion book to include a strong conclusion.

My Learning Goal

I can write an opinion book.

Use Capitalization

Every sentence needs to begin with a capital letter. The word **I** is always a capital letter.

MY TURN Edit the capital letters in these sentences. Write the correct words.

1. a dog is my favorite pet. _____

2. This is what i think is the worst pet. _____

3. frogs might hop out of a cage. _____

MY TURN Write a complete sentence on a separate sheet of paper. Remember to begin the sentence with a capital letter.

Conjunctions

Conjunctions are words that can join words or thoughts. The word **because** and the word **and** are both conjunctions.

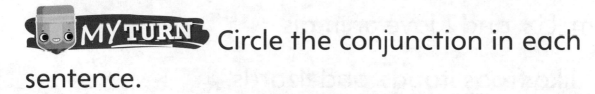 **MY TURN** Circle the conjunction in each sentence.

I think a fly is the worst pet because it is so small. Flies are tiny and are not fun to play with.

MY TURN Revise your opinion book to include at least one conjunction.

Commas

Commas separate words in a list.

 MY TURN Add commas where they are needed in each sentence.

1. Sam Liz and I love animals.

2. We like frogs toads and lizards.

3. We find them near ponds under leaves or by rocks.

MY TURN Add a sentence to your opinion book that includes a list. Remember to add commas where they are needed.

I can write an opinion book.

Edit for Conjunctions

Remember that conjunctions join words and thoughts.

> I like owls. They have large eyes.
> I like owls because they have large eyes.

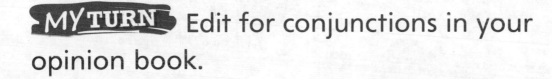 **MY TURN** Choose the better conjunction. Write **and** or **because** to complete each sentence.

I like butterflies _____ bees.

One reason I like them is _____ they fly near flowers.

MY TURN Edit for conjunctions in your opinion book.

Edit for Commas

Commas are used to separate words in a list.

> My kitten is smooth, soft, and fuzzy.

MY TURN Add commas to the correct place in each sentence.

1. Lions tigers and leopards are all big cats.

2. They are large strong and can roar.

3. They can be found in Asia Africa and in other parts of the world.

MY TURN Edit your opinion book for commas.

Assessment

You have learned how to write an opinion book.

 **MY TURN** Read the list. Put a check next to what you can do.

☐ I can write about a topic.

☐ I can state an opinion clearly.

☐ I can supply reasons that support my opinion.

☐ I can write an introduction and a conclusion.

☐ I begin each sentence with a capital letter.

☐ I use commas when writing a list.

☐ I use conjunctions correctly.

How to Use a Picture Dictionary

You can use a picture dictionary to find words. The words are grouped into topics. The topic of this picture dictionary is **categories**. Look at the pictures, and try to read the words. The pictures will help you understand the meanings of the words.

This is a picture of the word.

This is the word you are learning.

turtle

TURNand**TALK** Find the word **summer** in the picture dictionary. Name the other words in the same category. Use the words in sentences.

Categories

Colors

green

orange

purple

blue

Transportation

car

motorcycle

boat

helicopter

Animals

hen

giraffe

turtle

walrus

Seasons

spring

summer

autumn

winter

How to Use a Glossary

A glossary can help you find the meanings of words you do not know. The words in a glossary are in alphabetical, or ABC, order. Guide words at the top of the pages can help you find words. They are the first and last words on the page.

> All words that begin with the letter T will be after Tt.

> The word is in dark type.

Tt

temperature The **temperature** is how hot or cold something is.

> This sentence will help you understand what the word means.

TURN and TALK Talk with a partner about how a glossary in a book is different from a digital resource.

Aa

autumn Autumn is the season between summer and winter.

Bb

breeze A **breeze** is a light, gentle wind.

Cc

chilly If the air is **chilly**, it is cold.

crisp If the air is **crisp**, it is cool and fresh.

Dd

daylight Daylight is the light during the day.

Read Together

dry • process

dry When something is **dry**, it is not wet.

Ee

expect If you **expect** something, you think it will probably happen.

Ff

fawns **Fawns** are young deer.

Ii

information **Information** is the facts or details you get about someone or something.

Pp

process When you **process** information, you take the information in and use it.

Rr

rain **Rain** is the drops of
water that fall from clouds.

Ss

seasons The **seasons** are the four periods
of a year.

sense A **sense** is one of the five ways in
which you know what happens around you.
Touch, taste, smell, sight, and hearing are
the five senses.

snows When it **snows**,
white bits of frozen water
fall from the sky.

spring **Spring** is the season between
winter and summer. It is the season
when plants begin to grow.

squirrels **Squirrels** are small animals with bushy tails that usually live in trees and eat nuts.

summer **Summer** is the warmest season of the year between spring and autumn.

sunlight **Sunlight** is the light that comes from the sun.

Tt

temperature The **temperature** is how hot or cold something is.

Ww

weather The **weather** is the condition of the air outside at any given time. It includes information about temperature, sun, rain, wind, and so on.

winter **Winter** is the coldest season of the year between autumn and spring.

worms **Worms** are small, crawling animals that have soft bodies and no legs.

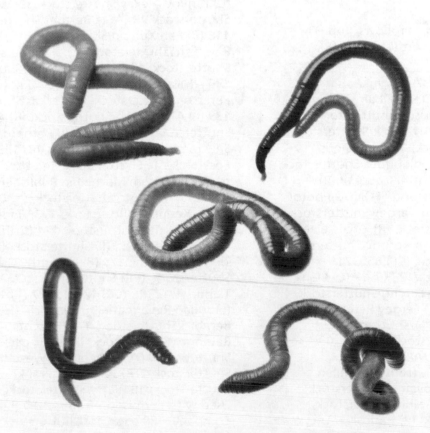

Text

ABDO Publishing Co.
Signs of Winter by Colleen Dolphin. Copyright ABDO Publishing Co.

Capstone Publishers
Excerpted from *The Ant and the Grasshopper* by Mark White. Copyright ©2012 by Capstone. All rights reserved.

Henry Holt & Co.
Every Season by Shelley Rotner & Anne Love Woodhull, reprinted by Henry Holt Books for Young Readers. CAUTION: Users are warned that this work is protected under copyright laws and downloading is strictly prohibited. The right to reproduce or transfer the work via any medium must be secured with Macmillan Publishing Group, LLC d/b/a Henry Holt & Co.; *My Autumn Book* by Wong Herbert Yee, reprinted by Henry Holt Books for Young Readers. CAUTION: Users are warned that this work is protected under copyright laws and downloading is strictly prohibited. The right to reproduce or transfer the work via any medium must be secured with Macmillan Publishing Group, LLC d/b/a Henry Holt & Co.

Photographs

Photo locators denoted as follows Top (T), Center (C), Bottom (B), Left (L), Right (R), Background (Bkgd)

4 Yanikap/Shutterstock, Art-Sonik/Shutterstock; **6** (Bkgd) Dean Fikar/Shutterstock, (BL) S. Borisov/Shutterstock; **7** Yanikap/Shutterstock, Art-Sonik/Shutterstock; **11** Jan Miko/Shutterstock; **12** (B) Smileus/Shutterstock, (Bkgd) kcablephoto/Shutterstock, (T) Robert Schneider/Shutterstock; **13** (B) Catalin Petolea/Shutterstock, (T) WDG Photo/Shutterstock; **14** (C) Ivan Karpov/Shutterstock, (L) Kim Reinick/Shutterstock, (R) Eric Isselee/Shutterstock; **15** (BL) Ivan Karpov/Shutterstock, (BR) Antpkr/Shutterstock, (CL) 650371/Shutterstock, (CR) Isselee/123RF; **17** (C) Elena Blokhina/123RF, (L) Zhu Difeng/Shutterstock, (R) Blotty/123RF; **19** (BL) Sergey Peterman/Shutterstock, (BR) 427411/Shutterstock, (CL) Zhu Difeng/Shutterstock, (CR) ER_09/Shutterstock; **24** HABRDA/Shutterstock; **26** Used with permission from Macmillan Publishers Ltd.; **53** Happyalex/Shutterstock; **56** (Bkgd) Andrey Mertsalov/Shutterstock, (C) Palasha/Shutterstock, (B) Radoslaw Lecyk/Shutterstock; **57** (L) Suiraton/Shutterstock,

(R) Leonid Andronov/Shutterstock; **58** (L) Mimadeo/Shutterstock, (R) Aksenova Natalya/Shutterstock; **61** (L) Avava/Shutterstock, (R) 123RF; **63** (B) Goodluz/Shutterstock, (C) Avava/Shutterstock, (T) Brocreative/Shutterstock; **68** Evgenia Tiplyashina/Fotolia; **71** (B) Yanikap/Shutterstock, (T) Art-Sonik/Shutterstock; **72** (Bkgd) Smit/Shutterstock, (T) Art-Sonik/Shutterstock; **73** Skynesher/E+/Getty Images; **74** Tomasz Wozniak/Shutterstock; **75** Yanikap/Shutterstock; **76** David Sacks/Getty Images; **77** Yukmin/Getty Images; **78** Jason Edwards/National Geographic/Getty Images; **79** ImageBROKER/Alamy Stock Photo; **80** Richard Ellis/Alamy Stock Photo; **81** Richard Ellis/Alamy Stock Photo; **82** (BCR) Arve Bettum/Shutterstock, (BR) chudtsankov/123RF, (TCR) Wolkenengel565/Shutterstock, (TR) Noomhh/123RF; **94** (B) Maxslu/Shutterstock, (Bkgd) Seanbear/123RF, (C) Studio 1One/Shutterstock, (T) Sbworld8/123RF; **95** Khakimullin Aleksandr/Shutterstock; **96** (C) VictoriaKh/Shutterstock, (L) Karkas/Shutterstock, (R) Jag_cz/Shutterstock; **97** (C) VictoriaKh/Shutterstock, (L) Karkas/Shutterstock, (R) Jag_cz/Shutterstock; **99** (C) Kirillov Alexey/Shutterstock, (L) Windu/Shutterstock, (R) Arve Bettum/Shutterstock; **118** (B) Pan Xunbin/Shutterstock, (C) Drew Rawcliffe/Shutterstock, (T) Clari Massimiliano/Shutterstock; **126** Zeljko Radojko/Shutterstock; **130** Africa Studio/Shutterstock; **132** (C) Richard Peterson/Shutterstock, (L) Karkas/Shutterstock; **133** (L) ATU Studio/Shutterstock, (R) Anythings/Shutterstock; **135** (C) Gerald Bernard/Shutterstock, (L) Shutterstock, (R) 123RF; **142** Epsylon Lyrae/Shutterstock; **144** Used with permission from Macmillan Publishers Ltd.; **172** (L) JHVEPhoto/Shutterstock, (R) David Byron Keener/Shutterstock; **173** Vladimir Chernyanskiy/Shutterstock; **174** (C) Timothy Geiss/Shutterstock, (L) Shutterstock, (R) Vitalii Tiahunov/123RF; **175** (BL) Timothy Geiss/Shutterstock, (BR) Shutterstock, (CL) Vitalii Tiahunov/123RF, (CR) 123RF; **177** (C) 123RF, (L) Julian Rovagnati/Shutterstock, (R) Gerald Bernard/Shutterstock; **179** (BL) Carsten Reisinger/Shutterstock, (BR) Eric Isselee/Shutterstock, (TL) TunedIn by Westend61/Shutterstock, (TR) Jeffrey M. Frank/Shutterstock; **184** Jarry/Shutterstock; **186** Used with permission from ABDO Publishing Company; **188** Luca Flor/Shutterstock; **189** Jochen Kost/Shutterstock; **190** George